How to Demonstrate Software
So People Buy It

by Brian Geery

HOW TO DEMONSTRATE SOFTWARE SO PEOPLE BUY IT
BRIAN GEERY

Published by SalesNV
Sarasota, Florida

ISBN: 978-0-9977779-0-1
LCCN: 2016914832

Contents

Reader Reviews

"Bad software demos kill even the most qualified deals. Brian's book breaks through the *sales book clutter*, bringing together an invaluable collection of stories, best practices and tips focused on one thing: closing more business by delivering great software demos. Every executive, every manager, every pre-sales engineer and every rep who sells B2B software needs to read this book."

Eric Blumthal, CEO, count5

"This book is spot on regarding the emphasis on selling solutions to the purchasing team members' pain points, rather than selling the wonders of software or hardware features and functionalities. If you want to sell more software, read this book."

Ed Heon, CEO, DATAgility, Inc.

"Thank you for putting together such a well-needed book on how to sell software. It could take a person just entering sales their entire career to learn the best practices of selling software that you share in your book, but by then it would be too late to put them into effect. I particularly enjoyed the format of detailing the key steps in the software sales process and how they were bookended with *What you can do today* in order to better integrate the lesson into one's sales approach. This book should become a trusted reference for those just starting out in software sales *and* seasoned pros."

Brian Slater, lifelong software sales pro

"Easy to read, good detailed information, specific steps to take. Excellent."

Beverly Flaxington, Principal, The Collaborative (three-time bestselling and gold-award winning author)

"In *How to Demonstrate Software So People Will Buy It*, Brian Geery masterfully articulates the strategies that define the art of transforming your software demonstration into the personal narrative of the prospect that sits before you. A must read for those sales professionals who want the recipe for the *secret sauce*."

Tom Modeen, lifelong software sales pro

"Buy this book! Do it now. I wish I had it 20 years ago. I lost a lot of sales over a lot of years learning the techniques, tactics and strategies Brian clearly explains here. I love this book! It should be required reading for every software sales professional, from beginner to seasoned pro."

Jeff Turner, VP Sales, Brightleaf Solutions

"This book is a must read for anyone who desires to be successful in software sales or selling any product requiring demonstration. You will become a better salesperson or a better sales manager with the benefit of Brian Geery's insights and methods which he skillfully articulates in his new book."

JoAnne Guarino, COO, ZetroZ

"As a software sales executive for over 20 years, I've observed how consistent top producing software salespeople always take care of the details, before, during, and after a demonstration to maximize the impact. This book lays out those details in an easy to follow, entertaining manner. Read the book, apply the strategies, and you will get larger commission checks."

Robert Conrad, VP Sales, EXALEAD

"Brian really understands the difference between your average, run-of-the-mill software demos and ones that improve your ability to close more deals. As a consultant, I've seen poor demos be the reason why deals are lost. I've also seen Brian's techniques in action and they work. If you're serious about increasing your win rate, BUY THIS BOOK NOW!"

Mike Scalcucci, VP, Business Development, Mainsail Strategic Consulting

Acknowledgments

Special thanks to Tom Modeen, my first mentor in software sales. Lessons I learned from Tom are dispersed throughout this book, including one real story about his software sales prowess (where he kicked my butt).

Thanks to Joanne Guarino, Dave Guarino, Mike Fabiaschi, Steve Swantek, Ed Heon, and Kathleen Fortin for being early influencers on my career and enabling me to be a top producer in software sales.

Thanks to Mom and Dad for teaching me about discipline and the importance of a positive attitude. (Mom took care of the positive attitude. Dad took care of the discipline.)

Thanks to Ingrid Bens for her guidance on self-publishing, writing in general, enthusiastic encouragement, and being the model writer I aspire to be. Check out Ingrid's books (when you finish this one) for guidance on how to facilitate a meeting. Your sales calls will be more productive.

Thanks to Cindy Readnower, my publicist extraordinaire. Once I completed the content, Cindy managed all the publication decisions. If I attempted to do what she did, the book might be out-of-date by the time it was published.

Thanks to Bob Leonard for editing the grammar, content and flow of this book. His *marketing guy* perspective enhanced so much of this book. He applauded, reworded, deleted, or questioned original versions. It's way better now.

Thanks to Robin Wrona for world-class copyediting. Talk about detail orientation. Wow. Robin fine-tuned the grammar, spelling, sentence, punctuation, and word usage. She also provided developmental editing ideas.

Thanks to the following people who have influenced the success of my career without knowing it. They are industry pundits, former coworkers, clients, prospects, networking contacts, colleagues, and top producers I have interviewed specifically for this book, or just plain good friends:

> Bob Conrad, Brian Slater, Christine Purnell, David Bowman, David Skok, Eric Blumthal, Eric Shoemaker, Frank Watts, Gerhard Gschwandtner, Jeff Gore, Jeff Turner, Kjell Purnell, Maria Pulsoni, Mark Engelberg, Matt Dragner, Michael Neece, Mike Scalcucci, Nathan David, Raymmar Tirado, Rich Swier, Rosemary Verri, Sally Sweeney, Scott Raskin, Steve Snyder, Teanna Spence, Terry Monteith.

Thanks to a ton of other people too: peers, bosses, sales leaders, clients, prospects who bought my software and even those who didn't! I can't list you all, but you know who you are. You taught me invaluable lessons about selling software. Like the time I was literally escorted out (hand on shoulder) of a sales call. Or the time I arrived late, dressed in casual clothes, for an appointment with suited bankers. Or the time I… (but I digress).

You all rock. There is no way I would have the privilege of crafting this manuscript without you.

Introduction

Demonstrations are the defining moment in the software sales process. When a software demonstration fails, everyone loses.

This book teaches you how to deliver software demonstrations that succeed.

Weak demonstrations cause software companies to lose millions of dollars annually. This means that salespeople lose thousands in commissions, and prospective customers lose when they fail to choose the best software solution to meet their business challenges.

Your product development team can create awesome software that helps your target customers increase revenues, reduce expenses, save time, *and* improve customer service.

Your marketing team can fill the top of your sales funnel with qualified prospects.

However, if your software demonstration is not persuasive and compelling, your close ratio will be low, your cost of sales will be high, and your sales cycles will be long. You will lose sales you should have won.

Jim Walsh, Chief Sales Officer of a high growth software company, was losing too many sales. He summed up his frustration when he told me, "We're spending all this money on product development and marketing... and it's working. We have a strong pipeline of qualified prospects, but when we demo our software, customers lose interest."

I asked if I could sit in on their next prospect demonstration.

Many aspects of the presentation were strong. The prospect was pre-qualified, the pace of the demonstration was fine, the salesperson was knowledgeable about the industry and the software, the benefits of the software were stated as each feature was demonstrated, and the application seemed easy to use.

Despite that, the overall demonstration was weak. Basically, the presenters were making five common, yet avoidable mistakes:

1. The demo wasn't memorable. Nothing in it made a lasting impression. After the presentation, when the purchasing team members discussed the various software solutions they had seen demoed, they could easily confuse this software solution with others they had seen. With no clear winner, they would likely make a decision based on price.
2. Two members of the purchasing team weren't present for the demo. Their peers would have to tell them about it – filtering their comments through their own interests and biases, making it likely they would not truly understand the software's value. Alternatively, another demonstration would have to be scheduled – wasting time and delaying the decision.
3. They were showing people how to use the software instead of persuading them to buy it. It was more like a training session than a sales presentation. There were not enough connections tying the software's functions and benefits to the prospects' daily challenges. There was no contrast between

the status quo and how much better life would be when they owned the software.

4. Nothing was said about the software's compelling advantages over a known primary competitor.
5. No business case justifying the cost of the solution, no proof points, and no discussion of the return-on-investment (ROI) were included.

When your software demonstration correctly addresses these five factors, your prospects will get excited about owning your company's software. Not only that, they will be eager to advance to the next step of their buying process.

This book will enable you to fine-tune your software demonstration, *including pre and post demonstration activities*. It will show you how to fix software demonstration issues like the ones Jim was grappling with.

Is this book for you?

- Is your demo-to-close ratio less than six out of 10?
- After your software demonstration, do prospects remain stuck in your sales funnel?
- Do you often have to deliver multiple software demonstrations to clear up misconceptions or misunderstood capabilities in order to close the sale?
- Do you think your competitors are winning the sale more often than you are because you are being "out-demoed?"
- Would you like to be in a stronger position when prospects start negotiating price?

If you answered yes to any of these questions, read on. This book will teach you how to fix your demonstration problems and enable you to sell more software, in less time.

Whether you sell six figure complex enterprise software, lower cost point solutions, software as a service (SaaS), platform as a service (PaaS), brand new applications, staid solutions, new versions of old applications, on-premises software, freemium software, middleware, or hardware appliances... this book is for you.

Whether you are a software company CEO, CFO, sales executive, marketing executive, product development executive, sales director or manager, pre-sales engineer, sales operations person, sales trainer, inside salesperson, field salesperson, or channel salesperson... this book is for you.

What's in it for you?

- Executives will have confidence that every software demonstration created or recrafted using the guidelines in this book will be delivered professionally, resulting in higher demonstration-to-close ratios.
- Managers, sales operations and sales enablement teams will possess a framework for training and coaching salespeople to deliver persuasive and

compelling demonstrations, as well as a process for continually improving the demonstration.

- Salespeople will earn more commission by delivering kick-ass, on target demonstrations that win sales.

Where did the content come from?

This book is a guide to best practices that will enable you to sell more software.

In my 30+ years in software sales and consulting, I have worked with countless CEOs and sales leaders at technology companies to fine-tune their teams' software demonstrations and increase demo-to-close ratios.

I have witnessed hundreds of salespeople delivering software demonstrations. There are times when I have seen prospects sitting at the edge of their seats with interest and enthusiasm, ready to buy. More often, I have seen prospects lose interest, get bored, and ultimately leave with no urgency, or worse, no motivation to buy.

In addition to my non-typical perspective, attained by observing so many software demonstrations, I've interviewed top producing software sales professionals to learn what they do that average sellers don't. I've learned how top sales professionals deliver persuasive and compelling software demonstrations that make their prospects want to buy immediately.

It is common for top producing software sales professionals to achieve demonstration-to-close ratios of 60% or more. That's six out of ten demonstrations ultimately concluding in a sale!

How to Demonstrate Software So People Buy It reveals what the most successful pros do and how you can do it too.

What's inside?

This book delivers an easy-to-follow map that will lead you to software demonstration success. Follow this map and your company achieves and exceeds sales goals, your salespeople receive larger commission checks, and your competition cringes when prospects mention your company's name!

This book is divided into four parts.

Part One – Pre-demonstration

> Stop! Before you demonstrate your software, you *must* do these pre-demonstration activities. If you do, your demo-to-close ratio *will* improve.

Part Two – Delivering the software demonstration

> Follow this formula: start with a James Bond opening, make the demonstration memorable throughout, solve prospects' pressing business challenges, justify the cost, and take out the competition.

Part Three – Post demonstration activities

> You can win the sale post demonstration – or lose it. Perform these post demonstration activities and you will tilt the scale in the right direction.

Part Four – Best practices of top producers

> Top producers practice their own art-of-the-sale. Do what these top producers do and you'll be one too.

You can scan the book by reading the *Executive Summaries* included at the start of each chapter, or you can read top producer stories that comprise most of each chapter. In these real-life stories, top software sales pros discuss how they *demonstrate software so people buy it.*

Every chapter concludes with a *What You Can Do Today* section. These sections include strategies that you can implement as soon as *today* to start improving your software demo-to-close ratio.

A process, not an event

Improving your software demonstration-to-close ratio is a process, not an event. This book includes scores of strategies for improving your demonstrations. Some strategies require time to implement, or trial and error to perfect.

Start by selecting a few strategies from the scores of strategies presented in this book and ease them into your sales day.

You may find yourself thinking, "Sounds good, but not going to happen; I don't have time." Resist this thinking. As you practice these strategies, they'll save you time and effort. Over the course of your next 20 or so software demonstrations, you'll have evidence that the time you invested in leveraging these strategies pays off. You will be accelerating prospects through their purchasing process and closing more sales.

The art-of-the-sale

Maybe you've experienced this seeming contradiction. Your company has three consistent top producers on its sales team, yet all three use different selling styles. It happens often.

I refer to this as the art-of-the-sale.

The art-of-the-sale is personal. It develops over time. Developing your own art-of-the-sale style enables you to make decisions on the fly that advance the sale. You know when to put the pen in a prospect's hand and make him sign, when to call out a purchasing team member for his opinion, how to respond to objections, when to discuss competitors, or when to walk. You *read the deal*, and respond accordingly.

The art-of-the-sale takes place when you are preparing to have a conversation or are in conversation with a prospect. It's where you blend your personal style with sales lessons you have learned. The art-of-the-sale is similar to a fingerprint; no two are identical. Top producers continually develop and refine their art-of-the-sale.

One top producer I met put it this way, "It's all about the narrative and a conversation. Are they feeling it? Are you reaching them?" He compared his art-of-the-sale style to a shadow boxer. Like the boxer, he's always ready for his prospect's next move.

I'll be covering many successful software selling strategies in this book. I'll call out ones that I know require applying your own art-of-the-sale.

Some recommended strategies may not match your personal art-of-the-sale. If that is the case, try to blend the strategy into your personal style. If anything really feels awkward, look for the essence of the strategy – what is the objective of the action? Tailor the strategy by putting your own spin on it.

Remember that many of my recommendations are likely new to you. Don't discount them out of hand. Try them, even if they're outside of your comfort zone. That's what top producers do. They try everything and then figure out a way to make them part of their own art-of-the-sale.

Note about characters and companies in the book

All the success stories described in this book are based on real salespeople in real selling situations. Their names have been changed, except in a few situations where I want to give credit to my mentors.

I also chose to keep the names of software companies anonymous; I just state the type of software that the company sells.

Part One – Pre-Demonstration

Chapter 1. The importance of pre-demonstration planning

Executive summary

- Careful pre-demonstration planning wins the sale.
- Truly understand your prospects' business challenges *before* scheduling your demonstration.
- Failing to do pre-demonstration planning, is planning to fail.

Chapter details include the following:

1. Three real-life stories of top software sales pros discussing real-life prospects and how pre-demonstration planning enabled (almost) all of them to win the sale.
2. Consequences versus benefits comparison table, illustrating the importance of pre-demonstration planning.
3. The significance of calculating your demo-to-close ratio so you can track improvement (and size of your commission check!).

Just show me the software!

"Just show me the software!" Teresa's prospect, Ken Mattis, VP of Marketing commanded.

Because their time is so limited, it is common for prospects like Mr. Mattis to be eager to see your software. They are reluctant to *waste time* engaging in a conversation about their situation. They figure that if they just see the software, they can determine if it's what they need.

They're wrong and you would be too if you just show them your software.

Teresa, an inside salesperson for a Software as a Service (SaaS) marketing solution, responded authoritatively, "Ken, it is vital that I understand a few things about your current situation before I show you the software. Otherwise, we'll waste a lot of time going back and forth to find the features and benefits that are most important to you."

Like Teresa, you need to sell your prospects on investing some time up front to discuss their business challenges.

Teresa, a top producer, knew that if she *just showed Ken the software* without a better understanding of his marketing challenges, she would diminish the probability of winning a sale. The demonstration would likely conclude with Ken saying, "Looks good. I need to think about it."

Without knowledge of *Ken's* marketing challenges, Teresa would not be able to deliver a persuasive and compelling demonstration that resulted in a sale (or at least a commitment to the next step of Ken's buying process).

Unless your software is a simple point solution to a single problem, it will offer a variety of features and functionality. For example, assume you are selling software that solves business challenges for wholesale distributors of plumbing supplies. How do you know whether to focus your demonstration on solving counter service problems, delivery truck routing problems, or accounting problems?

Or, what if you are selling software that solves business challenges for physician practices? How do you know whether to focus your demonstration on solving insurance billing problems, patient scheduling problems, or medical records problems?

In Teresa's case, Ken may have had marketing challenges with search engine optimization, management reporting, website design, buyer transactions, content marketing, or something else. Without knowing Ken's priorities, Teresa risked missing the mark during the demonstration, or boring Ken by showing him every feature.

It is imperative to not, "Just show me the software!"

Pre-demonstration planning enables you to understand your prospects' day-to-day business challenges, and then create a strategy to demonstrate how your software solves those challenges.

Why you should never skip pre-demonstration planning

Adam Burns is a top producing software sales professional, usually.

He works from his home office in Salt Lake City for a global company that sells molecular modeling software to scientists at universities. Adam returned from a ten-day President's Club trip to Maui and immediately dove into his sales pipeline on Monday morning. There was a lot of work to be done!

On Thursday, Professor Schmidt, a scientist at the University of Utah, requested a software demonstration for the following Tuesday. Adam responded, suggesting they wait a week so that he could do his pre-demonstration due diligence. But Professor Schmidt was insistent. He had all the right colleagues available on Tuesday. While Adam was away, the university had secured a grant. They were in a position to make a purchase decision.

Adam had been working on this opportunity for seven months. During that time, he had met with several of the professors who would be using the software, including Professor Schmidt who was a key decision maker and his primary contact. Adam felt he understood their needs. They were interested in using the software for life and material science predictive analytics, chemical inventory management, and integrative therapeutics.

However, Adam was concerned because he had never spoken with Professor Lane, the Provost; or James Ellington, the Academic Computing Director; both of whom would be present on Tuesday.

But, hey, they were anxious to buy and they had money! Adam acquiesced.

Adam had a general understanding of the Provost's and Computing Director's typical needs. He had learned their likely responsibilities a few years earlier during new hire training, and he had met numerous people with similar titles since. He figured he'd do his best to show them how the relevant features solved their challenges.

During the in-person demonstration, which was scheduled for an hour and a half, Adam noticed Provost Lane glance at his watch on several occasions. Then, after an hour, the Provost excused himself to take a phone call. When he returned, he said, "Hey team, I've got to deal with an emergency situation. Let's debrief at Monday's meeting." He turned to Adam, thanked him for his time and was out the door. Not a good sign.

Flash forward. Adam lost the sale.

During his post demonstration debrief conversation with Professor Schmidt, Adam learned that Ellington (the Computer Director) felt all of the different software solutions they had previewed would work. They all had the security and integration functionality required by the IT department.

However, Provost Lane, the ultimate decision maker, was delighted with how the primary competitor's software managed laboratory planning, operations, and resource management. Although most Provosts rarely cared about these types of features, at the University of Utah, responsibility for planning, operations, and management fell squarely on Provost Lane's shoulders. His interests were different from the typical Provost's. He was enamored with the competitor.

Had Adam known, he could have focused on Provost Lane's needs as well, or even scheduled a separate demonstration to review the functionality that was more relevant to him. The sad fact is, Adam's software had valuable features in those areas that the winning competitor's software did not!

In hindsight, Adam realized he lost the sale *before* the demonstration. He could have simply said, "No." to a Tuesday demonstration. Or, he could have persuaded Professor Schmidt to insist that Provost Lane have a 20-minute discovery dialogue with Adam before the demonstration. Then Adam could have precisely addressed the Provost's needs, demonstrated his software's competitive advantages, and won the sale. But *could haves* earn no commission checks.

Pre-demonstration planning prevents you from losing sales. Don't skip it.

You can win or lose *before* the demonstration

Elisha McManus is a top producing sales professional. She sells e-learning software, which is designed for companies that have a high percentage of work-from-home employees. Her software ensures that remote workers are always up-to-date with product knowledge.

Elisha's primary competitor sold software that could accomplish the same objectives. The competitor had been in business longer. It had brand recognition. It had more customers. Its price was competitive (sometimes even lower).

Additionally, the competitor's software was feature rich. During demonstrations, Elisha knew that her competitor highlighted the software's features and superior functionality.

By comparison, Elisha's software was new to the market. It got the job done with a number of important features, but at this stage of development, it was relatively *no-frills*.

Elisha was invited to demonstrate her software to Takaden, a manufacturer of custom-made office furniture. During her pre-demonstration planning, Elisha discovered that Takaden was interested in new software because it was introducing three new product lines. Its employees were located in home offices around the world. The new furniture was high tech and would require Takaden's employees to learn detailed product knowledge in order to explain the benefits as compared to its competitors.

If Elisha had *not* done pre-demonstration planning, she would *not* have known the following:

- The CEO was an early adaptor of technology and a user interface fanatic. He hated software that was not intuitive. He also ran the business by the numbers, always slicing and dicing data.
- The Vice President of HR was retiring in two months. The HR Director was taking over for the VP of HR. His primary responsibility was to ensure all employees were competent about the new product lines. His performance goals were aggressive. Most importantly, he needed validation that employees had learned what they had been taught.
- The Director of Training was a, *Yes, Boss* guy with no decision making authority.
- The CFO didn't need an ROI or business case. He already had his own.
- The Director of IT was similar to the CEO. He wanted the latest, greatest technology.

Because she had access to tracking data, Elisha also knew that the entire purchasing team was well-informed about her software; everyone had seen the generic software demonstration on her website. Some had clicked through and watched more detailed videos.

At this point, Elisha told her Sales Manager, "I've got them right where I want them."

Because Elisha did her pre-demonstration planning, she was armed with information that enabled her to plan a winning strategy. Elisha was confident she would win the sale *before* she even delivered the demonstration!

Here is how Elisha planned her winning demonstration strategy:

- Ask the CEO to take control of the mouse so he can experience firsthand the intuitiveness of the user interface for executive reporting and key performance indicator (KPI) dashboard creation. While the CEO is *playing*, explain that her company was founded on the premise that it could leapfrog competitors by using new software development tools. Tools that enabled software developers to create experiences like the CEO was having. The software was clearly easy to use, with no instruction or learning curve.
- Explain how her product development and marketing team do market research to identify all the latest, greatest software development tools and programming methodologies. Then, offer to run pilot projects with existing customers to validate the tools and methodologies' usefulness for training remote workers. Point out that Takaden would gain a competitive advantage by always leveraging the latest technology. The competitor's software can't keep up because it is an older design with fewer application programming interfaces (API). For example, only her software can leverage gamification and integration with social media, both proven to decrease employees' learning time and improve retention.
- Demonstrate to the HR Director the built-in training validation features, emphasizing the benefits. Tell real life stories about how her existing customers' productivity metrics improved because of learning validation functionality. During her customer success stories, Elisha shows a slide that illustrates a customer's KPIs before and after using her software. The graphs (displaying dollars, numbers, or percentages) were impressive!
- Avoid detailed feature descriptions since everyone had seen the basic demonstration on the website.
- Acknowledge the Director of Training and VP of HR throughout, but limit conversation time so that she can spend more time in conversation with the decision makers.
- Acknowledge the CFO's ROI and confirm that he still believes there is a solid business case for purchasing the software.
- Refer to her software as *industrial strength* and explain that it is designed to run a business and avoid distracting employees with superfluous whiz-bang features. Emphasize that her software is rock solid compared to software that could have bugs because of too many whiz-bang features.
- Explain her company's product development prioritization strategy, including how some *nice-to-have* features were *not* on the short term product development roadmap. Those features had been researched and deemed to have no real impact on customers' businesses. Explain how fluff features look good in a demonstration, but in real life that's all they are, fluff. Similar to the knobs on a high end stereo, they look cool, but they are rarely, if ever, used.

Because of her pre-demonstration planning, Elisha knew precisely what to show to whom and how to position her software against the competition. Elisha's competitor was set up to lose the sale. Elisha was set up to win the sale. She did.

When you master pre-demonstration planning, you often know that you will win a sale *before* you even deliver the demonstration.

With or without pre-demonstration planning

Rushing to the demonstration with no pre-planning, is like being a pilot and failing to perform your preflight checklist. You risk disaster. Too many times I've observed software demonstrations where I could read the prospects' mind, *Excuse me. Relevance?* That's not what you want them thinking.

Here is a summary of the consequences of foregoing pre-demonstration planning compared to the benefits of pre-demonstration planning.

Without pre-demonstration planning	With pre-demonstration planning
Confusion about which features to demonstrate to whom	Deliver compelling, persuasive, and targeted demonstrations
Unable to discuss the business case for purchasing	Present ROI / business case
Stumped by objections	Anticipate and remove objections before they come up
Unknown decision makers kill the deal	Address each demonstration participant's unique needs
Not clear on next step in purchasing process	Gain commitment to next steps
Lose upper hand to competitors	Present competitive advantages
Can't forecast accurately	Predict size and time of commission check

What should your demonstration-to-close ratio be?

To keep it simple, a *demonstration* in my *demonstration-to-close ratio* can represent one demonstration or multiple demonstrations to the same prospect.

I hesitate to use an example because some of you sell more complex enterprise solutions and others sell less expensive point solutions. Please use this example and apply the math to *your earnings situation*.

To keep the math simple, let's say you currently close three sales out of 10 demonstrations. You average 50 demonstrations per year. You earn $5,000 in commission per sale, which adds up to $75,000 in annual commissions on top of your base salary.

By following the principles in this book, you increase your demonstration-to-close ratio to five out of 10 demonstrations. Now you earn $125,000 in annual commissions. That's 50,000 more bucks in your pocket. Not bad.

What should your demonstration-to-close ratio be? There is no one right answer and many variables affect your close ratio. However, based on my experience working with countless software companies, if you are closing less than six out of ten demonstrations, you can likely improve your demonstration-to-close ratio – and increase the size of your commission check.

Another benefit, as you improve your demonstration-to-close ratio, you will also reduce the number of demonstrations needed to close a single sale.

So the answer to what your demonstration-to-close ratio should be, "higher than it is now!"

Effective pre-demonstration planning is a critical element of improving your demo-to-close ratio. It is a key distinction between consistent quota achievers and average salespeople.

What you can do today

> Calculate your current software demo-to-close ratio. It will be fun to watch it improve as you apply the strategies in this book.

Chapter 2. To demonstrate, or not to demonstrate

<table>
<tr><td align="center">Executive summary</td></tr>
</table>

- It is imperative to define your top-tier prospect.
- All prospects need to be assessed and compared to your top-tier prospect definition. *Are they a reasonable match?*
- Not all prospects are equal, so don't treat them that way. Walk from opportunities with those who do not reasonably match your top-tier prospect definition.

Chapter details include the following:

- o Two methods for defining your top-tier prospect, *the ideal world way* and *the quick and dirty way.*
- o Defining and comparing a prospect's *reasonable match* to your top-tier prospect definition; variables that need to be considered, including a real-life story that illustrates how a top producer assessed two prospects against her top-tier prospect definition.
- o Examples of top-tier prospect definitions you can use to create your own, including a real-life conversation about why one quota smashing overachiever walks from non-top-tier prospects.

Select your prospects carefully

My pride and joy is a 1988 Mercedes. It may not be the most economical sled on the road, but it's my indulgence.

On a recent visit regarding a maintenance issue with Chris Connelly, a 25-year veteran mechanic who only works on Mercedes, he told me about an eye-opening experience he had a few years ago. "Brian," he said as he lowered his chin and shook his head, "the customer is not always first."

Chris' revelations are important to us software sales pros. I'll tell you why in a moment.

Chris explained that for years, when he worked at a dealership, he was taught that the customer is always first. When he started on his own, he ran his repair shop that way.

One day he serviced a cantankerous customer who claimed the parts and labor costs were extraordinary. Chris did his best to explain why, but ended up giving a discount because of his *customer first* mentality.

Chris had spent hours diagnosing the problems, researching the cost of replacement parts, determining a repair plan, and fixing the problem. He told me after giving the discount, "I could have made more money working at McDonalds."

Chris' revelation that day was that his customers were not always first. *His time* was first. Servicing the wrong customers was not only wasting Chris' time, but it was an opportunity cost. Every minute Chris spent servicing the wrong customers was a minute he could have been servicing top-tier customers.

Chris realized that he could choose to spend his time working with top-tier customers, whom he characterized as those who were reasonable, appreciated his work, and had no problem paying for his service. Since his revelation, Chris has not hesitated to tell other complain-in-the-pants customers or customers whose repair jobs were not in his area of expertise that their work was not for him.

Chris smiled when he said, "Now I let my competitors get stuck with unprofitable work or challenging customers." He said that watching those customers drive away is like watching stress leave his world. By not wasting his time on those customers, Chris now makes more money than he used to, his work is less stressful, and he enjoys his customer relationships.

Top producing software sales professionals are similar to Chris. Before delivering a demonstration, they assess potential sales opportunities carefully. They question whether those opportunities possess characteristics that are similar to the characteristics of existing great customers. Top producers are willing to walk away from opportunities that are likely to waste precious sales minutes because prospects balk at the price or make no decision at all. Or worse, they buy the software and become nothing but trouble for the customer service or finance teams.

Wesley Ianovale, a top producer who sells property management software, put it this way, "If I'm not going to earn a commission check, I'd rather stay at home with the family or go fishing than spend my time working my ass off for no commission check."

Like Chris the mechanic, Wesley learned from experience. After delivering software demonstrations to dozens of prospects, and losing many sales, Wesley had his own revelation. He realized that fear of losing a potential commission check was driving him to demonstrate to *any* prospect who raised his hand and expressed interest. What Wesley had failed to understand was that the *opportunity cost* of spending his precious sales minutes with marginal prospects should drive his behavior, not fear of loss.

With his revelation in mind, Wesley thought carefully about the opportunities he had won and lost. Using this information, he defined his top-tier prospect. He identified the characteristics of those opportunities that closed frequently and fast.

Armed with this information, Wesley started managing his sales minutes more selectively. He assessed each prospect's situation more judiciously. He carefully decided if and when to demonstrate his software. When he changed his approach of rushing to demonstrate, he earned larger commission checks and was consistently ranked at the top of the leaderboard.

By carefully assessing all of his prospects against his top-tier definition, Wesley became willing to walk away from or delay demonstrating to unqualified prospects.

Wesley would have conversations where he told his prospects who were interested in property management software the following:

> "It's important to determine if you can download your resident data files before we schedule a demonstration. That will change the features and functionality you need to see."

> "Since your IT department doesn't allow remote support, our software is not for you."

> "Let's wait to schedule a demonstration until the people who manage your rent roll and your building maintenance can attend. If they are not on board, you won't be able to make a confident decision."

> "Our software is designed for commercial property management. Because you have so many residential properties included in your portfolio, we are not a match for you."

> "If you don't need to manage multiple commercial properties, our software may be overkill for you."

Wesley was polite and honest. Prospective customers were appreciative.

Wesley felt like Chris the Mercedes mechanic. By gracefully declining to pursue the customer relationship, he was able to invest his sales minutes working with top-tier prospects.

You too will sell more software by being selective about the use of your sales minutes. Select your prospects carefully.

The importance of a top-tier prospect definition

As I hand you a dart, I say, "Aim for the bull's-eye."

You look around the room. Then you give me a puzzled look, "Ah, where's the dart board?"

You can't hit the target, let alone hit the bull's-eye, if you don't know where the target is.

Similarly, in the profession of sales, in order to sell to your *bull's-eye* customer, you have to know what the definition of that customer is. I call it your *top-tier prospect* definition.

Here's a simple way to identify your top-tier prospects. During your initial conversation, assess whether the new prospect has similar characteristics to past prospects where you were able to make the sale quickly, without competitive battles or discounting your price.

Defining your top-tier prospect enables you to focus your sales efforts those prospects who have the highest propensity to buy. When you stay focused on pursuing top-tier prospects, you have more accurate forecasts, you develop the most profitable customer relationships, and you earn the biggest commission checks.

How to define your top-tier prospect

There are two ways to define your top-tier prospect, the ideal world way and the quick and dirty way.

In an ideal world, you would engage a team of busy executives in a series of meetings.

In a quick and dirty way, where you simply don't have time or executive interest, you invest an hour a month for three months or less.

Read both ways and develop an approach that works in your situation.

One: the ideal world way

Defining your top-tier prospect is relatively easy, but it will take multiple meetings and consensus gaining with a variety of participants within your company.

Multiple meetings are necessary because defining your top-tier prospect is an evolving process.

Consensus gaining is required because different constituents will see things through different lenses. Some participants may feel a certain top-tier prospect's attribute is more important than another; for example, some participants may feel a top-tier prospect must have already established a budget. Others may feel a top-tier prospect must be up against a timeline. Some participants may feel there are certain types of prospects not worth pursuing.

Five steps to defining your top-tier prospect definition:

1. Assign a team leader
2. Identify participants
3. Facilitate consensus gaining meetings
4. Create and distribute final definition
5. Assign definition updater

Step One, assign a team leader

Make one person accountable for completing your top-tier prospect definition. This Team Leader is typically from the marketing team, but every company is different. Select a person who has an expertise facilitating meetings, has an understanding of the dynamics of your organization structure, and has a record of getting things done.

Step Two, identify participants

Must-include participants in creating your top-tier prospect definition are the following:

- Top producing salespeople (field, inside, and/or channel)
- VP Sales
- VP Marketing

Optional participants include:

- CEO
- CFO
- CTO
- Product development executive
- Sales director or manager
- Pre-sales engineer
- Sales operations person
- Sales trainer
- Customer service

And any others whose opinion is deemed relevant!

Step Three, facilitate consensus-gaining meetings

Have your Team Leader schedule a series of brainstorming/consensus-gaining meetings to create a definition of your company's top-tier prospect. Your team leader should decide who is invited to the various meetings because all companies have different organizational and geographic structures.

Using a whiteboard or mind mapping software, the Team Leader should capture everyone's opinions during these meetings. Participants should be reminded that when brainstorming, all ideas are welcome.

Brainstorming

A group problem-solving technique that involves the spontaneous contribution of ideas from all members of the group.

— Merriam-Webster.com

During these meetings, agree up front that there is no such thing as a bad idea. The only bad idea is one that isn't verbalized. Also, agree that there is zero room for contentious interactions. You are a team who wants to accomplish the same goal: sell more, make more money. Everyone will be happy when that happens!

The characteristics that you identify run the gamut from company to company. Characteristics that you may want to consider for your company's top-tier prospect definition include the following:

- **Demographics**: US based? South America? Canada? Number of locations? Number of users?
- **Types of sale**: Business-to-business? Business-to-consumer? Channel?
- **Psychographics**: Personality traits of purchasing team members? Get into details or delegate? First time buyers? Been burned before?
- **Company**: Early adopters? Laggards?
- **Industry**: Manufacturers? Financial institutions? Healthcare?
- **Stage of growth**: Early stage? Funded? Pre-revenue? Dominant?
- **Status of sales**: Increasing? Decreasing? Stagnant?
- **Life cycle of products**: Prototype? First release? Staid?
- **Status of market share**: No market share? Some? Majority?
- **Competitor status**: Using a named existing solution? Competing against a particular competitor?
- **Compliance issues**: Legal requirements? Standards adherence (e.g. APIs, OSHA)?
- **Merging/acquiring**: About to merge or acquire? In midst? Acquired?
- **Outdated software**: License expired? Expiring? Capacity limited?
- **Downsizing**: Planning lay off? Laying off? Merging locations?
- **New product release**: Have a new product in release mode? Planning?
- **Decision maker profile**: Early stage in career? Tenured? Education level? Title?
- **Level of urgency**: Nice to have? Want to have? Need to have?
- **Company valuation**: Profitable and growing? In distress? Pre-revenue?

And any other characteristic you deem important!

In addition to capturing your top-tier prospect definition, sometimes it is useful to identify your non-prospects. Those are prospects who possess characteristics that make doing business with them undesirable or impossible.

You will find examples of top-tier and non-prospect definitions below.

Step Four, create and distribute final definition

After facilitating the meetings, the Team Leader drafts a top-tier prospect definition based on the consensus-gaining meeting outcomes. He then distributes it to the team and solicits *one* round of feedback.

I recommend no more than one round of edits from the group. It would be easy to edit, reedit, and keep reediting! Good is good enough.

Keep in mind, you'll never really have a *final* version. Your top-tier prospect definition will evolve over time. Let the sales team use it for a quarter. Then revise if need be.

Step Five, assign definition updater

All the above is not worth doing if you don't have a person designated to review and update your top-tier definition as needed on a quarterly basis. When changes are made, it is imperative that sales managers use the definition when performing pipeline reviews, so that salespeople aren't wasting sales minutes on prospects who are not a reasonable match to the top-tier prospects definition.

Two: the quick and dirty way

The quick and dirt way is used when you simply don't have time to use the ideal world way. Instead of corralling a team and leading a series of meetings, you do it yourself.

Schedule three one-hour meetings in your calendar over the next three months.

By yourself or with a few peers, review six of the most recently won sales and six of the most recently lost sales.

What are the characteristics of each? Where are the correlations?

Whiteboard or mind map your answers. Begin a list of what made the *wins* top tier and what made the *losses* below top tier.

Use this data to assess your existing pipeline and new prospects.

Repeat two more times over the next two months.

Reasonable match to the top-tier definition?

As a sales professional, your goal is to work only with prospects who are a *reasonable match* to your top-tier prospect definition.

While prospects are typically referred to as being qualified or unqualified, I prefer assessing whether prospects are a reasonable match when compared to a predefined top-tier prospect definition. I believe this makes it easier to manage your pipeline and prioritize where you spend your time. Here's why.

A reasonable match is defined by you. It is not black and white, like qualified or unqualified. The criteria can change depending on numerous factors affecting your overall sales pipeline. You have to assess the time left in the month or the quarter, the status against your sales goal, the overall quantity of prospects in each stage, and miscellaneous factors as you see fit, not the least of which is the size of your commission check. For example, a prospect you would pursue this quarter may be one you would not pursue next quarter because next quarter you have prospects that are *even closer* to your defined top-tier definition.

It is rare to find prospects who are a *perfect* match to your top-tier prospect definition. Should you find a perfect match prospect, no discussion. Lock and load!

How a top producer assessed *reasonable match*

Sandy Edwards sells software that enables marketers at large retailers to improve their web presence, which results in increased sales.

Below is Sandy's top-tier prospect definition. She assessed whether Prospect A or Prospect B was a more reasonable match using her definition. Here is how the assessment looked.

Top-Tier Prospect Definition	Prospect A	Prospect B
Retailers with $100M+ in sales	✓	✓
Ideal industries: internet retailers or ecommerce	✓	
Executive team is unified, improving SEO ranking is paramount	✓	✓
In process of evaluating SEO technology solutions	✓	✓
Need visibility into how online marketing initiatives are working (best when need visibility into a specific sales channel)	✓	
In exploratory mode because of impending renewal with a competitor	✓	✓
Competitors are beating them in keyword positioning		✓
Hit tipping point of doing SEO manually, it takes too much time		
New person hired to manage SEO		✓
Spending too much money on paid search or other lead generation channels	✓	✓
Redesigning website to improve organic search		✓
Need to sell seasonal items		✓
Have purchased SEO technology before	✓	✓
Focused on new customer acquisition	✓	✓
Can articulate the value of a new customer		✓
Has an SEO management process and a team focused on online new customer acquisition, ideally across departments		✓
Already generating online leads but wants to protect their asset		
Website has notable SEO problems	✓	✓
Red flags and non-prospects: • No budget for SEO and no other marketing budget to tap • Comprehensive international needs • SEO is a buzz word and want to learn more • History of using lower cost solutions (aka they are cheap) • Need convincing why SEO is important		

Assume you are Sandy. You are up against the end of the quarter. You only have time to work on Prospect A or Prospect B. Which one would you pursue?

If you selected A, go sit in the back of the class.

Prospect B possesses notably more characteristics of a top-tier prospect than Prospect A. Focus your sales minutes on Prospect B. Prospect A may be pursued beginning next month.

There is a caveat. Not all top-tier prospect characteristics are weighted equally. Some carry extra weight. You'll need to develop an approach to assessing *reasonable match* based on your selling situation.

The first step of pre-demonstration planning is to assess and evaluate prospects using your top-tier prospect definition.

Refer bad prospects to competitors

When prospects are not a reasonable match to your top-tier prospect definition, refer them to your competitors. Prospects will be grateful and your competitors will have to spend their time on those prospects while you pursue top tiers!

Examples of top-tier prospect definitions

Below are examples of top-tier prospect definitions from a variety of software companies.

Note the differences. Some top-tier prospect definitions are based more on demographics; others are more on need-based. Some are decision-maker-profile-based, yet others are more feature-requirement-based. Top-tier prospect definitions vary from company to company. Yours will be unique to your company.

Top-tier prospect definition – software to manage physician practices

A top-tier prospect for a company that sells software to manage physician practices:

- 20+ doctors
- 2+ locations
- Existing software at least four years' old
- Want online medical records, no resistance
- Desire to increase patient volume
- Improved patient scheduling is a driver of interest for new software
- Physicians believe marketing is important and understand they have to spend money on it
- Consensus that patient referrals from primary care physicians should not be their only source of new patients
- Office Manager has 5+ years tenure, at least two as Office Manager
- Treat more Medicaid and Medicare patients than private insurance patients

- Non-prospects: podiatry, optometry, dermatology, and cosmetic surgery practices

Top-tier prospect definition – software to manage field service personnel

A top-tier prospect for a company that sells software to manage field service personnel:

- Companies that need time and expense tracking and/or project and task management
- Need to bill for field service personnel work
- A new, defined project and service management business challenge (pain point) is driving interest
- CEO, CFO, COO and/or Dir. of Services or Professional Services are involved in the buying process
- Willing to develop an ROI model with us
- Willing to provide an organizational chart of users which includes names, titles, reporting relationships, areas of responsibility, and contact information
- Have a dedicated, full time, project manager for the implementation phase
- Have international locations
- 50+ users
- Use 3 or more disparate systems or spreadsheets to manage field service
- In one of these industries:
  - Consulting or Technology Services
  - Engineering Services
  - Architectural Design Services
  - Field Support and Service
  - Manufacturing Delivery and Setup
  - Software Development
- Industries not to pursue:
  - Legal
  - Hospitals
  - Accounting
  - Construction

Top-tier prospect definition – software to manage the process of writing software (software development kits)

A top-tier prospect for a company that sells software development kits (SDK):

- A developer who needs an SDK to add imaging capabilities
- Have a date sensitive *business* project with an approved budget
- CTO is engaged in project
- Have a business requirement that there are no client installs (aka thin client)
- Want to view scanned or faxed documents via the Web
- Need to view large format scans on the web, like scanned mechanical drawings, oil well logs, strip charts, or documents with many pages

- Want specific technology (e.g. royalty free bar code reading, annotating documents over the web, or PDF viewing)
- Have advanced imaging needs, including editing metadata, reading distorted images, rearranging TIFF files, cleanup old/bad scans, PDF reading, web annotations, or barcode reading
- Have many licenses of desktop deployments so want run time royalty free
- Located in North America, Western Europe or Australia
- Non-prospects:
  o Have mostly MS Office documents
  o Not .NET (e.g. PHP, Java, C++)
  o A non-Windows based server
  o Interested in Web Viewing, but using Java Server architecture
  o Building a desktop client application

Note that all three top-tier prospect definitions include a definition of prospects that are not worth demonstrating to.

Use these examples to create your own top-tier prospect definition!

Walking from a sale is not easy, but it is smart

David Bowman is such a top performer that when the company re-assessed its commission plan, it left David's sales figures out of the calculations. His figures skewed the averages. It was not uncommon for David to achieve his annual quota half way through the year.

David sells software to manage hotel chains.

I had the privilege of talking to David about his success. With his forecast in front of me, I said, "David, you have the Marriot Hotel chain on your forecast. Can you tell me about that opportunity?"

"Well, I called Bill Marriot," David responded.

With an incredulous look on my face, I said, "You what!? Bill is the Chairman of the Board. How did you get hold of him? What did you say?"

(How David reached Bill is another subject for another book.)

David said, "I told Bill that I was going to work numerous hours with his executive team and many of their team members. I know the importance of their time and I don't want to waste it. Whichever company you select to upgrade your automation will require an investment of millions of dollars and cause significant changes in how you operate your global business. I realize you will be involved in a decision of this importance. Is it okay if I call you occasionally during this process in order to get your input?"

To which Bill replied, "Good idea. Here is my direct line. I'll tell my assistant to put you through."

"And what would you have done if Bill had said *no* to your request?" I asked.

"I would have walked from the opportunity," replied David, matter-of-factly.

"You would have walked from a potential multimillion-dollar sale because the Chairman of the Board wouldn't talk to you?" I asked in amazement.

David responded, "I've learned from experience that it's extremely important for me to establish a relationship with the ultimate decision-maker as early as possible in the sales process."

David clarified, "I would have called on Bill a number of times before walking from the opportunity."

I felt better.

David continued, "There are many other hotel chains for me to call on. Each opportunity I decide to work with will involve a lot of my time because I am always selling to multiple purchasing team members. That means I can't be working on a large number of opportunities at the same time. So, I select prospects that have a higher likelihood of buying, and invest my sales minutes with them. If the ultimate decision-maker will not agree to take my calls, I don't have a high likelihood of closing the sale."

To this day, I'm not convinced I would have walked from that sale if Bill Marriott had said, "No," to me. Walking from a sale isn't easy. Salespeople work so hard to find opportunities that when one surfaces, it is natural to want to pursue it. However, I've learned that top producers walk away from more opportunities than average salespeople do. Hey, you can't argue with David's logic. Look at his numbers.

Make the decision not to demonstrate as soon as you identify a major issue that will mitigate closing the sale.

Remember Chris Connelly, the Mercedes mechanic, and Wesley Ianovale, the property management software sales pro? They learned the hard way that some prospects aren't worth pursuing.

Top producers and average producers have the same number of sales minutes in their day. Top producers leverage their sales minutes more wisely.

Note: I believe that all salespeople with some tenure in their role *know* when to walk. But they often don't. I'm guilty of the same behavior!

What you can do today

- Define your top-tier prospect.
- Assess the prospects in your sales pipeline using your definition.
- Determine if you have a reasonable match. Move forward with your sales process, or not, based on your determination.

Chapter 3. Pre-demonstration discovery

Executive summary

- Pre-demonstration discovery is a process of asking questions. It enables you to perform pre-demonstration planning so that you can deliver a persuasive and compelling software demonstration.
- *Selling* prospects on participating in your pre-demonstration discovery.
- Pre-demonstration discovery questioning is an ongoing process.

Chapter details include the following:

- o Pre-demonstration discovery objectives, time needed for discovery process, alternatives if thorough discovery isn't possible, and discovery tasks that may be optional.
- o A top producer's real life story about how he *sold* a prospect on participating in pre-demonstration discovery.
- o Examples of pre-demonstration discovery questions that you can use to create your own, including a top producer discussing how she prioritizes her pre-demonstration questions.

What is pre-demonstration discovery?

Discover

To see, get knowledge of, learn of, find, or find out; gain sight or knowledge of.

— Dictionary.com

Pre-demonstration discovery is a process of asking questions. It enables you to perform pre-demonstration planning so that you can deliver a persuasive and compelling software demonstration. Sometimes you ask questions during phone conversations, sometimes while meeting in person, other times via email.

Pre-demonstration discovery primes your demonstration for success.

The discovery process can be compared to the following:

- a scientist seeking the truth,
- a four-year-old asking, "Why?" "Why?" "Why?"
- a psychiatrist, saying, "Tell me about that."

The goal of pre-demonstration discovery is to get beyond the *Employees Only* sign to see what's really going on in the workplace. Usually, it isn't pretty compared to what life would be like if those employees used your software.

What is the objective of pre-demonstration discovery?

The pre-demonstration discovery process informs you about your prospects' reality today so that you can demonstrate how your software makes their reality tomorrow so much better.

The discovery process also enables you to build rapport with the purchasing team. You get to know people as people, not just employees. The relationships you develop can often give you a competitive advantage.

The objective of pre-demonstration discovery is to learn as much as you can, as quickly as you can, about four items:

1. Qualification – determine if your prospect is a reasonable match to your top-tier prospect definition.
2. Need – identify your prospects' pressing business challenge(s) and determine their sense of urgency to invest in software.
3. Purchasing team – identify the decision making team and learn its needs.
4. Purchasing process – understand your prospects' purchasing process.

How long does pre-demonstration discovery take?

The length of time your pre-demonstration discovery takes will vary based on numerous factors. If you are selling complex business application software that is used by multiple people and costs six figures, you'll need to invest more time in discovery mode than if you are selling lower cost software that is a point solution used by small groups or individuals.

One top producer put it this way:

> "The trick is for pre-demonstration discovery to take as little time as possible to get as much information as possible that is relevant to my software demonstration."

When selling complex software, it is often preferable to perform your discovery onsite. During that time, schedule a series of individual meetings and/or sessions to observe processes. This enables you to ask detailed questions about how prospects go about their business. Armed with this information, you can do a better job demonstrating how your software will improve their daily business lives.

When selling lower cost, point solution software, your discovery process will usually require only a 20-minute phone conversation (provided you get the answers you require).

When selling complex or point solution software, speak with as many purchasing team members as possible prior to your demonstration. If you can't speak with everyone, consider asking purchasing team members to complete an online questionnaire or simply respond to a few email questions.

Sell prospects on the discovery process

Often, you have to sell prospects on the idea of participating in a discovery process. Like Teresa's prospect, Ken Mattis, your prospects may not understand the value of this process. One of the reasons Teresa is a top producer is because she has mastered the art of convincing prospects to engage and participate in a discovery conversation prior to attending her software demonstration.

You have to persuade prospects that investing some upfront time will make the software demonstration more relevant to their unique business requirements and ultimately will actually save everyone time. You are the expert in delivering demonstrations; let them know you have learned how to do it in the most time efficient way.

Gene Tait, a top producer who sells software to manage prisons said, "Since my software is used by so many different departments, I have to speak with a lot of people during my discovery."

The software assists with prisoner intake, guard scheduling, inmate sentence tracking, kitchen and clothing inventory management, and vehicle maintenance. It ties information from all these departments together for the human resources and finance teams.

Gene explained that some people are reluctant to meet with him. In order to persuade them, Gene said, "I crafted an email template that explains the value of investing some time upfront to answer my questions. It worked great!"

Gene had two templates: one for his key contact, and one that could easily be forwarded by the contact to other people Gene needed to meet.

While his email is confidential, he shared that the core message describes how prospects will have a better demonstration experience by investing some time upfront to discuss how they do business today. His demonstration will be more efficient and productive. He'll be able to answer all of their questions. And, they will leave with clarity as to whether the software is the right solution for them.

Gene laughed, "But wait, there's more."

Gene explained, "When having the actual discovery meetings, I restate the reasons from my email. Otherwise, it would be easy for the conversation to feel more like an inquisition because I ask so many questions!"

In an ideal world, sales teams would have as much time as they wanted to perform their pre-demonstration discovery process, but it's not an ideal world. Prospects are busy people and often reluctant to spend much time answering your questions.

To be a top producer like Gene, *sell* your prospects on having a discovery conversation prior to seeing a demonstration.

Pre-demonstration questions must be prioritized

Sally Romens is a top producer who sells software that enables the design and administration of sales commission plans.

During her discovery process, Sally has learned that it is important for her to have a conversation with the CFO regarding his or her philosophical view on paying commission. Some CFOs want commission expense to be high because that means sales are up. Other CFOs have more of a penny-pinching mindset. They view salespeople as costly overhead. Other CFOs are somewhere in-between.

During a conversation with Sally about how she always exceeds her quota, she explained, "When I know a CFO's philosophical view regarding sales commissions, I can change how I position my software as a solution to her commission calculation challenges."

Smiling at its simplicity, Sally said, "I can demonstrate how my software enables her to design commission plans that motivate salespeople to generate revenue. Or I can demonstrate how my software enables her to design commission plans that control profit. Or however I need to demonstrate it – so that it matches her viewpoint."

"However," Sally continued, "It's not easy to get a CFO to have a conversation, and when he or she does, it is often rushed."

Sally said that her last two CFO meetings, which were scheduled for just 15 minutes, were cut short.

So, Sally carefully prioritizes her question list. "I assume that I'll only get to ask two or three questions. That forces me to think seriously about what those questions should be and how to prioritize them!"

Questions on her prioritized short list at the time of our conversation:

1. If you finish a year and feel very good about how your commission plan worked, what will have happened?
2. Why has purchasing commission management software become important at this point in time?
3. What functionality is most important for you to see during our demonstration?

Sally explained she has tried variations of these questions and the order in which she asks them. Through trial and error, she determined this list and the order of questions that works the best. Question one typically leads to a conversation where she learns the CFO's philosophical view regarding sales commissions – the most important thing she needs to understand to deliver a persuasive and compelling demo!

To be a top producer like Sally, it's imperative that you master your pre-demonstration discovery process.

Examples of software company pre-demonstration discovery questions

To make it easy for you to develop your own pre-demonstration discovery questions, I pulled a few examples from clients' master pre-demonstration question lists (see below).

These questions are based on the type of software application being sold. As you review these lists, you'll understand how answers to these questions impact the salesperson's software demonstration strategy.

Also, you will find other generic pre-demonstration discovery questions in the following chapters and a consolidated master list in the Appendix.

Your pre-demonstration discovery questions are *customized* to your selling situation. For example, a person selling real estate management software will want to know if his prospects manage residential or commercial real estate. Or a person selling software to manage libraries will want to know how many titles a prospective library carries. Unless you sold those specific software packages, you would never care about the answers to those questions!

Your master question list will emerge over time. How you prioritize your list will also evolve. To get started, just make a list; don't overthink it. Then try it out in the field and refine it as you go.

Master question list – when selling software to manage sales commissions

- Are reps paid on a salary plus commission?
- If commission only, is it paid monthly? Is it paid on cash receipts or bookings?
- If cash receipts, is your rate determined when the cash comes in the door?
- Define the sales crediting process – how do you determine who gets credit for the sale? What *value* does the salesperson get credit for?
- Does commission kick in only after goal is achieved?
- How do you define sales territories?
- Do you calculate or pay incentives in more than one currency or language?
- Are sales managers paid an override?

Master question list – when selling software to manage a recruiting process

- Describe the information gathering process once you begin a recruiting assignment. Who does what? What bottlenecks do you experience? What steps of the process are frustrating or time consuming? How would reducing the frustration and time required impact productivity?
- How often do you use personalized, mass emails to communicate with your network (clients, candidates, potential clients, etc.?) What process is in place and how long does it take? What bottlenecks do you experience? Would mass email campaigns be effective if you had the time? How would your business be impacted if you sent a personalized email to all your key contacts once per quarter?

- What tools do you currently have in place to maintain organized, consistent data? How are the tools working?
- Please rate your database for its integrity on a one to 10 scale, 10 being perfect. For any answer below a 10: What would it take to make it a 10?
- How does your firm share an updated list of all active search projects? What tools do you have to verify what each member has accomplished on a project or during a certain period? What percent of your time is consumed by these information-sharing tasks? What is the value of your time in dollars per hour?

Master question list – when selling software to manage a physician practice

- Do you need electronic medical records?
- Are you using a Windows platform?
- What areas of your practice would you identify as having workflow challenges?
- What requirements do you have for scanning?
- What common challenges do you incur with regard to remittance?
- Will you want any data converted from your old system to your new system?
- Any remote offices? If so, for what purpose?
- How do you do electronic posting?
- What percent of your patients are on Medicare?
- How much are couriers costing you? What courier challenges exist?
- How much are transcription services costing you? What challenges exist with regard to transcriptions?
- How much time (man-hours) is spent defending reimbursement rejections?
- What regulatory/compliance issues do you have?

It's worth noting that the majority of these questions are open-ended. They cannot be answered with a *yes* or *no*. When you use open-ended discovery questions, prospects provide richer answers.

Pre-demonstration discovery optional tasks

How far you go with your pre-demonstration discovery is up to you.

I've met top producers who do the following to enhance their discovery process:

- Read LinkedIn profiles and send invitations to connect
- Google purchasing team members' names
- List the company on their Google news alerts
- Scour their prospects' websites
- Scour their prospects' competitors' websites
- Read trade publications

I've also met top producers who do none of the above. They just engage in conversation.

Top producers do the legwork – they find the information they need.

My personal style is to learn as much as I can while being as efficient as possible with my sales minutes. It's surprising sometimes how much you can profit from a short conversation. Once I made a sale because I chatted with the prospect about his black belt status, which I learned by Googling his name!

Ultimately, your approach to researching your prospects will be subject to your personal preference, sales process, pipeline size, complexity of sale, etc.

What if you can't do pre-demonstration discovery?

Sometimes situations exist where you simply can't perform your pre-demonstration discovery. For example, if marketing produces an overabundance of leads or if you are selling lower cost, point solution software, you may have to demonstrate your software without having the time for a complete discovery process.

If this is the case, your demonstration may not be as persuasive and compelling as you'd like, but you can still win the sale by generalizing. You can demonstrate how to solve common business challenges. You can discuss common consequences of the status quo. You can deliver your competitive positioning message. And you can discuss a typical business case for purchasing your software.

After the demonstration, when a prospect indicates she is interested in next steps, you can perform follow-up strategies that lead to winning a sale.

High-velocity selling

Every year there are advances and innovations in the process of selling software. A relatively new approach to selling is referred to as *high-velocity selling*, which concentrates on leveraging marketing platforms, inbound marketing, content management, lead scoring, and inside sales teams. Additionally, it employs a plethora of technologies to streamline prospects' buying processes, reduce cost of sales, and increase overall production of sales and marketing teams.

When using a high-velocity sales system, the software demonstration may be the most important part of the process. It is a single point of failure.

> Single point of failure
>
> *A single point of failure is part of a system that, if it fails, will stop the entire system from working. SPOFs are undesirable in any system with a goal of high availability or reliability, be it a business practice, software application, or other industrial system.* — Wikipedia.com

You can implement a high-velocity sales system, but if your software demonstration is weak, it will stop the entire system from working. You will lose sales.

What you can do today

- Write down your pre-demonstration questions.
- Prioritize your questions from most important to least important.
- Field test your questions with your next prospects. Refine and reprioritize questions as needed.

Chapter 4. Why does your prospect need software?

Executive summary
• Determine the catalyst(s) for your prospects' interest in your software. Is there an urgency to purchase or will you need to develop a sense of urgency?   • If you have to develop urgency, your pre-demonstration discovery is more involved. You have to ask more questions.   • Building on prospects' catalysts for interest enables you to accelerate opportunities through your sales pipeline.   Chapter details include the following: ○ A fun quiz – assess prospects' level of urgency (including a real-life top producer story and his most important question).   ○ A list of questions that can be used to identify prospects' challenges and determine their level of need.   ○ Examples of trigger events that cause prospects to have interest in new software.

Assess prospects' level of pressing need

Prospects that are a reasonable match (based on your assessment) to a top-tier prospect definition are qualified. Schedule a software demonstration.

Next, ask yourself, *Are the prospects' needs pressing? Pressing needs* are business challenges that are "urgent; demanding immediate attention" (dictionary.com).

Like a second level of qualifying, understanding prospects' *pressing needs* for your software solution will help you determine how aggressively you should pursue their business. The less urgent and the less immediate attention your prospect's business challenges are, the less likely you will be able to make a sale.

Creating movement in your pipeline

Don't you hate it when you tell your manager that an opportunity will close *this* month, but it doesn't? The next month you tell him that the same deal will now close *this* month. But it doesn't.

It's embarrassing. It makes for small commission checks. It can cause you to fall off the leaderboard.

Lack of urgency is one of the most common reasons prospects become stuck in the sales pipeline month after month, or worse, quarter after quarter. If you can develop a sense of urgency, you can get your prospects *unstuck*. If you cannot develop a sense of urgency, movement through the middle of your sales funnel will continue to stagnate.

The more pressing the prospect's business challenge, the more urgency he will have to solve it. If your software does not solve your prospect's *pressing* business challenges, why should he buy it?

You are selling software to busy people who are managing multiple priorities. Their time is limited and their to-do lists are long. Their lists include pressing challenges that are negatively affecting time, money, personal satisfaction, or growth of the business. They need to increase revenue or reduce costs or both, all while keeping their customers, employees, bosses, and shareholders happy. And, there is a never-ending sense of urgency to address these challenges. This is their reality, which means they are not buying software because it's cool or nice to have!

One the contrary, they will gladly buy software that solves their pressing business challenges. Remember a need that is pressing requires, "urgent, demanding immediate attention." Prospects are dealing with numerous business challenges all day long. If the business challenge that your software solves is not pressing, if it is not on their short list to address, you are not likely to make a sale.

Catalysts for interest

Jason James is an inside sales professional. He qualifies and scores inbound leads for the Account Executive team at a company that sells software to manage legal firms. Jason continually ranks in the top five percent on the leaderboard.

I asked Jason how he does it. He said, "The most important thing I need to understand is why a prospect is interested in our software."

He continued, "And particularly, why *now*, at this point in time."

Jason said that one of the first questions he asks prospects who express interest in his software is, "'What causes you to have an interest in our software?'"

This question leads to a conversation about why new software is important *now*. Jason calls it the *consequences-of-the-status-quo* conversation. The more he can understand the consequences of a prospect not getting new software, the more accurately he can score the lead for his Account Executives.

Jason explained, "If a law firm secured a large new client, that's a better catalyst for interest than a law firm looking for new functionality that its existing software doesn't have. The former tends to have a pressing need for the software; the latter just wants it. The former has urgency to buy; the latter can get by as it is."

He summed it up like this, "When I understand a prospect's catalyst for interest, I understand his sense of urgency to purchase. I can tell my Account Executives where they are likely to make the best use of their sales minutes. They can only work on so many prospects at once, so understanding catalysts for interest enables them to prioritize opportunities most likely to close."

Can you assess these prospects' level of urgency?

Apply Jason's strategy to the above-mentioned top-tier prospect definitions. Which prospect would you score higher in terms of having a sense of urgency and a pressing business challenge?

Software to manage physician practices

You: "What causes you to have an interest in our software?"

Prospect A *and* Prospect B: "Problems scheduling patients."

You: "Why is this important at this point in time?

Prospect A: "We can't keep up. Patients are waiting too long to see their doctor. We have two new physicians and we are short on exam rooms."

Prospect B: "My Office Manager read a blog about patient scheduling and thought we should see what's new."

Prospect A gets a higher score as she has a more pressing need.

Software to manage field service personnel

You: "What causes you to have an interest in our software?"

Prospect A *and* Prospect B: "Need to bill for field service."

You: "Why is this important at this point in time?

Prospect A: "Our new CFO identified that we are not billing for all the time we should be"

Prospect B: "The spreadsheet we use is pain the ass."

Prospect A gets a higher score as he has a more pressing need.

Software development kits (SDK):

You: "What causes you to have an interest in our software?"

Prospect A *and* Prospect B: "Need to develop new software"

You: "Why is this important at this point in time?

Prospect A: "Our new website is going live on the 20th of next month. It requires viewing scanned documents.

Prospect B: "Our customer needs software developed for an upcoming tradeshow.

Prospect A and Prospect B get an *equally* high score as they both have a pressing need.

In addition to making the best use of your sales minutes and prioritizing opportunities most likely to close, understanding catalysts for interest and the associated sense of urgency enables you to be more authoritative in your conversations because you know the *why* behind their interest. Using this information, you can deliver a more persuasive and compelling demonstration and you can lead prospects through their buying process faster.

Questions to identify prospects' challenges and level of need to solve

Use these sample questions to develop your own pre-demonstration discovery questions.

Discovery Question	Reason for Question
How did you hear about our software solution?	Your questions and sales demonstration may change based on your lead source. For example, if the prospect was referred by someone he trusts, your conversation will be different from a prospect who found you via a Google search.
What causes you to be interested in our software solution at this point in time? *Depending on the answer, probe further: Why not wait six months? Why was this not so important six months ago?* *What would be the consequences if you do nothing and remain status quo?*	Identifies the level of urgency to buy your software.
Looking at the next two or three quarters, what are some of the other business initiatives taking place? *Where does investing in new software fall in importance compared to those initiatives?*	Further establishes level of urgency.

Please tell me about the business challenges that you would like to resolve.
 	
For each challenge, consider asking:
 	
  • *Tell me more.*
  • *How many people deal with that?*
  • *How long does it take?*
  • *What is the workflow?*
  • *How do you determine when the challenge is resolved?*
  • *How can we calculate the cost of this process?*
  • *If the problem went away, how would it help?*
	Enables you to demonstrate how to solve business challenges.
	
	Positions you as a consultative partner, not a vendor.
	
	Identifies the foundation for an ROI.
	
	Distinguishes you from competitors who do not ask these questions.

What type of information reporting do you need? *Why and when do you need it?*	Identifies which reports to demonstrate.

Do you need to develop urgency, or does it already exist?

Depending on your prospects' situation, you may be starting the conversation about a software purchase because urgency already exists. For example, they are up for an expensive software license renewal, so they want to make a decision whether to renew or purchase new software. Perhaps their existing support has become intolerable, or a new business process requires new software. Whatever the reason, when prospects have a predefined reason for urgency, you have less discovery work. They are purchasing new software; the choice is yours or your competitors'.

In situations where prospects don't have a predefined sense of urgency, you need to develop urgency during the discovery process. Begin by uncovering the consequences of the status quo.

For example, consider the situation above where a prospect's catalyst for interest in physician practice management software was, "My Office Manager read a blog about patient scheduling and thought we should see what's new," or the situation where the prospect's catalyst for interest in software to manage field service personnel was, "The spreadsheet we use is a pain the ass."

In both instances, the status quo could be considered tolerable. The prospect can continue running her business as it is. She can see your software, think it's cool, but decide not to prioritize purchasing it. She has other problems that are more pressing and the amount of money to spend is limited. If you want to make a sale in situations where the status quo can be considered tolerable, you need to perform a discovery process that produces information that you can use to *educate* prospects that the status quo is actually not acceptable.

Let's say you sell records management software. Your job is to reach out to companies or firms that most likely have records management challenges. In essence, *you* are the catalyst for interest. You don't have an inside sale pro like Jason on your team or a strong marketing engine generating leads.

Your prospect may be cruising along thinking life is good because she doesn't know about your software. Yet. You'll need to educate in order to sell.

Watch current events to identify and reach out to companies that are experiencing the following:

- Hiring
- Moving
- Merging or acquiring
- Experiencing litigation
- Growing fast

When you have your first time conversation with a prospect, you are probing to see if his company has challenges with the following:

- Capacity. No room for growing number of paper records storage boxes.
- Real estate changes. Moving and need to clean out paper records beforehand and organize at new location.
- Outsourcing initiative. Can't keep up with records management tasks internally.
- Purchasing issue. Purchasing team can't gain access to records fast enough.
- Recent incident. Had an audit or experienced litigation.
- Improve control. Experienced lost records or document security breaches.

Once you identify a records management challenge, you need to ask questions that reveal prospects' frustrations (a.k.a. problems and challenges) with the way things are being done today. Have a conversation about the consequences those frustrations have on time, money, personal satisfaction or business growth. Strive to identify the consequences in terms of dollars, numbers, or percentages.

The more dissatisfied prospects feel about the status quo, the more likely they will be to buy a solution that brings about change. Dissatisfaction is a powerful motivator.

Both types of prospects can be good. When prospects have a catalyst for interest, they are in buying mode and your sales cycle will be faster. When you help prospects recognize that they have a business challenge that your software can address, you have less, or sometimes no, competition. Your consultative approach causes prospects to want to purchase from you.

Trigger events

Events can trigger the need for software. In the example above, when selling records management software, the trigger events were hiring, moving, merging or acquiring, experiencing litigation, or growing fast.

I've seen trigger events run the gamut. Here are some examples:

- Regulatory changes
- License expiration
- Legal compliance
- Cost overruns
- New products
- Broken machines
- New executive
- Reorganization
- International expansion
- Competitor that keeps winning
- Data access inaccessible

I once worked with a top producer who sold software to manage inventory liquidation. Her catalyst for interest was unusual. She sold to companies that were going out of business.

What trigger events cause prospects to need your software? How can you identify when those trigger events happen?

Always have the catalysts for interest conversation

I'll call them Dr. Smith and Dr. Jones to protect the guilty.

One top producer I met, who sells physician practice management software, told me he was selling software to Dr. Smith. When he had a discussion with the doctor about his catalyst for interest, he discovered the real reason (true story) was that his colleague, Dr. Jones, had just bought new software. Dr. Smith wanted better software than Dr. Jones had. In fact, he even wanted to pay a little more and get some extra features so that his software would upstage his colleague's.

Have the catalyst for interest conversation with all prospects. You never know

---

What you can do today

- Use the examples of pre-demonstration discovery questions to create your own question set.
- Review all prospects in your short-term pipeline and assess their reason for interest. Is it pressing?
- If your prospects' needs are not pressing, meaning no real urgency to buy, focus your sales efforts on developing their needs.

Chapter 5. Who are the purchasing team members?

Executive summary
A purchasing team member profile consists of five elements, plus some optional elements to consider. The five elements include the following: 1. Titles and responsibilities 2. Day-in-the-life-of 3. Role in the purchasing process 4. Relevant software features and benefits 5. Communication styles Creating purchasing team profiles enables you to do the following: • Demonstrate the most relevant features and benefits of your software to each person (what's relevant to one person is irrelevant to the next). • Explain how each person's life will be better when he or she owns your software. • Communicate in a manner that each person will understand and appreciate. Chapter details include the following: o Ways to identify each of the five elements of your purchasing team members' profiles, and what to do when you can't. o Six top producer stories, in their own words, about experiences leveraging purchasing team member profiles in the sales process (and why some were successful, and some were not). o An example of a purchasing team member profile that you can use to create your own profiles. o Detailed descriptions of the five elements of a purchasing team member profile, plus optional elements to consider.

How and why to profile purchasing team members

One top producing software sales professional I met referred to his purchasing team profiles as a *roadmap to commission*. Another referred to her purchasing team profiles as a *green, yellow, and red light*. And yet another referred to his as a *heat map* of the sales opportunity. I've heard people use *buyer personas* or *decision maker profiles* as well.

No matter what you call it, a purchasing team member profile enables you to do the following:

- Demonstrate the most relevant features and benefits of your software to each person.
- Explain how each person's life will be better when he owns your software.
- Communicate in a manner that each person will understand and appreciate.

Five elements of a purchasing team member profile

There are five elements of a purchasing team member profile:

1. Titles and responsibilities

   When you understand the titles and responsibilities of each purchasing team member, you can easily adapt your sales conversations to software functionality that rings true to each person and supports her role in the purchasing process.

2. Day-in-the-life-of

   When you understand your purchasing team member's day-in-the-life-of, he becomes predisposed to purchasing from you because you can empathize so well with his specific circumstances.

3. Role in the purchasing process

   When you identify each purchasing team member's role in the purchasing process, you can be sure to provide him with the information he needs in order to make a *yes* decision.

4. Software features and benefits

   When you prepare to demonstrate relevant software features and benefits to each purchasing team member, your demonstrations are more efficient and your close ratio increases.

5. Communication styles

   When you understand each purchasing team member's communication style, you can converse in a way that matches his preferred manner of communication.

If you want to sell more software, you can't overestimate the value of creating a profile for each purchasing team member.

How to identify purchasing team members

Manuel Vasquez sells software to manage legal firms. He is a top producer. Manuel was discussing how he identifies purchasing team members after he knows the company is a reasonable match to his top-tier prospect definition.

"I build rapport with my primary contact, gauge his role in the purchasing process, and understand his responsibilities," Manuel said.

These are examples of the questions he asks:

- How long have you worked at the company?
- How did you come to work here; did the company find you or did you find the company?
- Please tell me more about your responsibilities. What is your role in the software purchase process?
- Have you led the software purchasing process previously, here or at other companies?
- What software functionality will be most important to you?

Using what he learns from these questions, he asks his primary contact for assistance understanding who's who in the purchasing process.

Manuel told me, "I was taught to ask my primary contact, 'Who else is involved in the purchasing process?'"

He explained that this simple question enabled him to identify purchasing team members. However, the question didn't insure that he knew who *all* the purchasing team members were. It posed two problems.

First, some primary contacts would hear the words *who else* as, "Who are the *real* decision makers, you minion?" They would become defensive and say, "Just me."

So Manuel changed the wording to, "Who, *including you*, is involved in the decision making process?" This simple change prompted accurate answers, not defensiveness.

Manuel's sales manager told me that one of the reasons he is a consistent quota achiever is because he sweats the details. Refining a simple question to make it more effective is one example!

Second, some primary contacts actually don't know or are not willing to disclose the names and titles of the purchasing team members.

Manuel said, "I know the likely titles of purchasing team members that should be involved in buying my software. So I often have to ask my primary contact a few questions."

He gave me examples of his questions:

> "I noticed that you haven't included anyone from your Business and Intellectual Property Litigation team. Who will be assessing that functionality of our software?"

> "Law firms I work with, that are similar in size to yours, often want someone from their Licensing or Strategic Relations team to review our contract. Who will review our contract at your firm?"

Manuel also learned, the hard way, never to assume a purchasing team member's role in the purchasing process. He's lost sales by not understanding purchasing team members' responsibilities and what level of authority they had regarding purchasing software. Once, he had a self-professed decision maker have to *take it to committee* before purchase. Another time an IT team member, who identified himself as a decision maker, could only sign off on security, not application integration.

"I've learned to ask my primary contact to tell me each person's role on the purchasing team." Manuel told me that he could point to a number of sales he closed because he had the answer to this simple question.

Jason James, the Inside Sales Pro mentioned earlier, said that with his prospects, someone from the IT and/or the Legal team were often left off the purchasing member list. These two questions help him identify the other members:

> "I noticed you haven't included anyone from IT in this process. Who will determine if our technology matches your IT team's specifications?"

> "Many customers I've worked with need their legal teams to review the paperwork. Who will review the paperwork from a legal perspective?"

Asking questions like Manuel's and Jason's early in your sales process prevents surprises later. Nothing is worse than thinking you've made the sale only to find out there's one more person who has to sign off!

Attempt to speak with all purchasing team members

In an ideal world, prior to your software demonstration, you'd have an opportunity to speak to each purchasing team member for as long as you need.

It's not an ideal world.

You can, however, have brief conversations with most, if not all, purchasing team members.

Leverage your relationship with your primary contact. Ask her, "Will you please arrange for me to have a ten-minute conversation with each of the purchasing team members? These brief conversations prior to the software demonstration will enable me to know what participants are most interested in seeing and avoid wasting anybody's time."

Keeping these meetings brief will demonstrate respect for people's time, while still giving you the opportunity to establish rapport with key decision makers and gain an understanding of their personal business issues. As a result, you will be empowered to deliver a more compelling demonstration.

During these conversations, ask just three questions:

1. Please tell me about your key responsibilities.
2. What is the most important aspect of this new software to you? Why?
3. Compared to other important business initiatives you are managing over the next few quarters, what is the relative priority of implementing this new software?

These three simple questions will provide you with invaluable information so you can deliver a more effective demonstration.

Note: be sure to watch the clock and adhere to your promise of a ten-minute meeting. Or, ask permission to go overtime if necessary.

Some software requires that you spend more time with certain purchasing team members. You may need an hour or two to learn about processes, view existing software, or delve into details about the overall business. Remember – if you can't schedule these important conversations, you may need to postpone the demonstration!

I can hear some of you now: "Great idea, but my demonstrations already take too long. If I spend more time having individual conversations with decision makers, I won't be able to perform enough overall demonstrations." In reality, you will find yourself spending less time per demonstration because you are focused on demonstrating only what prospects really want and need to see.

1. Titles and responsibilities

Speak to me in dollars

During my career as a sales manager, I once approached my CFO seeking budget approval for an investment in technology. I thought the technology would help my salespeople sell more.

Shortly into the conversation, my CFO raised both his hands with his palms facing me. "Stop," he commanded.

I responded with a puzzled look.

He said, "Speak to me in dollars and numbers."

I asked to reschedule.

Three days later, I came back with a return-on-investment presentation. I explained how we could pilot the technology with six salespeople for under $5,000. During the three-month pilot, I would track revenue generated directly as a result of the technology. I presented the worst case (we waste $5,000) and why it was unlikely, and then I presented the best case (we win three or more sales worth $50,000 each) and why I thought it was likely.

"Now you're speaking my language," my CFO cheered me on. He approved the expense.

I thought, *Duh, Brian! Do ya think you could've figured that out before you walked in here the first time?*

Based on the Chief Financial Officer title, I should have known he would need to understand the business case for any expenses. If I had done my pre-presentation (aka demonstration) planning, I would have connected the dots. Budget request…Chief Financial Officer…hmm, present ROI!

Presuppose prospects' responsibilities based on their titles

When you know someone's title, you can make deductions regarding his or her responsibilities. (Note, it is important to validate these deductions during your conversations. Remember Adam selling to the Provost?) As in the example above, I could have deduced that a CFO would be interested in a cost/benefit analysis.

These title descriptions are straightforward. You can easily make suppositions about the following titles and the likely responsibilities that a person with that title would have.

Title: Chief Executive Officer (CEO)

Responsibilities:

- Company revenue and profit
- Shareholder or investor goals
- Employee relations
- Executive team development
- Make sure no one messes up!

Title: Chief Financial Officer (CFO)

Responsibilities:

- Profit
- Expense management
- Profit and loss (P&L) and income statement
- Bank relations
- Accounting

Title: Chief Marketing Officer (CMO)

Responsibilities:

- Brand
- Quantity of qualified leads generated for sales
- Website
- Ecommerce
- Search engine optimization and pay-per-click advertising

Create your own title and responsibilities list

Titles and responsibilities vary based on the type of software you sell. For example, here is a title and responsibility list for a company that sells software to manage bed capacity at hospitals:

Title: Chief Medical Officer

Responsibilities:

- Direct the staff and programs of the hospital's medical and nursing programs. Work closely with hospital staff, department directors,

and physicians to ensure that the highest standards of quality and service are maintained.
- Serve as a mediator between physicians and hospital executives. Physicians want new equipment, expensive staff, modern facilities, food bars, and the ability to manage their own schedule. Hospital executives want physicians to refer patients for hospital services, adhere to hospital procedures, prescribe the correct drugs, and keep costs down.
- Ensure quality of care and regulatory compliance.
- Mitigate liability and medical errors.

Title: Chief Nursing Officer (CNO) or Vice President of Nursing

Responsibilities:

- Administer hospital nursing program to maintain standards of patient care.
- Advise medical staff, department heads, and administrators in matters related to nursing service.
- Recommend establishment or revision of policies and develop organizational structure and standards of performance.
- Hire, train, and schedule the nursing team.
- Track treatment outcomes, patient flow, patient safety, and length of stay.

Title: Hospital CIO or Director of Information Systems

Responsibilities:

- Set long-range direction of the hospital's technology. Direct the strategic design, acquisition, management, and implementation of hospital technology infrastructure.
- Oversee a plethora of different systems. Identify what should be purchased, what should be upgraded, when and how integration happens, and compatibility issues.
- Maintain technology standards for the organization.
- Direct the activities to keep the technology infrastructure running seamlessly, efficiently and effectively.
- Ensure compliance with legal and medical standards.
- Stay current with ever-changing government regulations.
- Prevent security issues.

Use the above examples to create a title and responsibilities list that matches the prospects in your pipeline.

Software interests by title within functional area

During your software demonstration, tailor your conversations with titles within the different functional areas of the company to target their needs.

For example, if you are selling software that helps the marketing department, different titles will have different interests. Marketing Assistants, SEO Practitioners, Marketing Managers, Brand Managers, Merchandisers, Directors of Marketing, VPs of Marketing, and CMOs all have different needs for your software.

When I sell my firm's consulting services to fine-tune software demonstrations, I know the following:

> CEOs want a scalable sales process that delivers predictable revenue.
>
> VPs of Sales want improved software demonstration-to-close ratios.
>
> VPs of Marketing want sales and marketing alignment.
>
> Sales Operations Directors want time and budget to support the demonstration efforts.
>
> Salespeople want a software demonstration process that enables them to win more sales.
>
> CFOs want return-on-investment of sales organization costs.

So my conversations with each person in each functional area will be different. They will be focused on typical wants and needs of the title or functional area.

(Yes, that was a blatant plug.)

Selling software to mid-level management

If you are selling software to mid-level managers or directly to an employee, interests by title within functional areas are especially important. Your buyers will need to sell internally on your behalf. They may think your software is awesome, but if upper level management doesn't buy in to the value proposition, you will not sell your software.

Some purchasing team members are detractors

Staying with the example of selling records management software, the purchasing team typically consists of these titles:

- Vice President of Finance
- Operations Manager
- Records Manager

The VP Finance and Operations Manager may be enthused about your software because of inventory control features, records retrieval service, access security, and cost savings.

However, the Records Manager may see your software as a threat to his job. Of course, he would never tell anyone this, but he certainly could resist the purchase and raise objections.

It is important to recognize that some purchasing team members may have a catalyst for interest and sense of urgency to purchase new software, yet others (by nature of their role at the company), may be predisposed to not want your software.

2. Day-in-the-life-of

One of the most valuable sales training lessons I learned was during my new hire training at Turn & Earn Systems. The company sold software to manage electrical wholesale distributors. My new hire training agenda included visiting existing customers and observing how they used our software.

My sales manager gave me a list of a few questions to ask each person with whom I met. He told me to be sure that I met the president of each of our customers' businesses. Presidents were always a key decision maker on the purchasing team in our market.

One question on the list for presidents was, "What caused you to buy our software?"

I met with six presidents. Without fail, their answers to my *what caused you to buy* question were, "Ed Heon."

I prompted them to go further. They explained, "Ed knows my business." I subsequently observed Ed, the founder of Turn & Earn Systems, giving an in-person software demonstration.

After introductions, Ed discussed the reason that Turn & Earn Systems exists.

He would turn to the president and say, "Picture a fine golf day. You're having a beer after the front nine. You glance at your phone and see this dashboard." Ed showed a PowerPoint slide of the dashboard. "We call it the turn and earn report because it enables you to turn the most inventory."

Inventory turns are a key performance indicator in the wholesale distribution business. The report prioritized inventory items that were turning well, or not so well. It was graphic and easy to interpret.

"Here's what you do next. In a few clicks, you give kudos to your executive team regarding these performance highlights," Ed said while showing a color-coded key performance indicator dashboard. Green, yellow, or red indicated high to low turning items.

Ed continued with enthusiasm, almost as if he was on the golf course, "Then, in one click to Patrick in the warehouse, you highlight overstock of Sylvania A100's. In one click to Jimmy, your product manager, you highlight shrinking margins on Hubbell 5252's and add a note about looking into Belden instead. And it's on to the back nine."

After a pause to let them digest what he said, Ed continued, "One of our newest customers, I'll refer to them as Hendricks Electric as this is confidential information, went from 4 to 5 inventory turns in two quarters, a one-time cash savings of $1,000,000."

Ed showed them this spreadsheet and said, "Here's what happened."

Hendricks Electric

Cost of Goods Sold	$20,000,000
Total Inventory Value (average)	$5,000.000
Days of Inventory	91
Inventory Turns	4.0
Annual Carrying Cost	$1,000,000
Cash Tied Up in Inventory	$5,000,000

Increase turns by 1	
Inventory Turns	5.0
Days of Inventory	73
Annual Carrying Cost	$800,000
Annual Carrying Cost Savings	$200,000
Cash Tied Up in Inventory	$4,000,000
One Time Cash Savings	**$1,000,000**

(This table is not Ed's original; it is from in an article in *Industrial Supply Magazine* by Howard Coleman titled "Four Inventory Turns Per Year Doesn't Cut It Anymore!")

I watched Ed's performance on multiple occasions. I'd swear that after the discussion about how increasing inventory turns generates more free cash flow, the president was ready to buy.

Ed knew about the *day-in-the-life-of* a president of an electrical wholesale distributor. Most would prefer not to be in the warehouse managing inventory every day. Most sold Sylvania, Hubbell, and Belden products. All had challenges with overstock and margin control. And what president doesn't understand that cash is king?

Like Ed, when you have conversations with your prospects, make them feel like they are speaking with a peer, someone who understands what they do for a living.

Ed spoke the language of the CEO of an electrical wholesaler. He knew his business. He understood his and his employees' daily life and what they needed to accomplish. Ed knew what they needed to succeed. He understood a day-in-the-life-of.

If you understand your prospects' business, speak their language, and relate to their pressing business challenges, you will be able to connect the dots between your software and their reality. And you will close more sales.

Of note. One day I took a tour of a prospect's warehouse with Ed and the CEO. They stopped here and there to talk about a particular shelf of inventory. I didn't understand much of what they said.

Afterwards, while Ed and I were driving back to the office, I asked him, "How do you know about all that inventory?" I knew Ed never actually worked in the electrical wholesale distribution business. He was in the software development business and gained his expertise working with a few electrical wholesale distribution customers.

Ed said, "I have no idea what's in the boxes."

"*What*?" I said, incredulously.

He smiled. "Brian, I learned some common products and part numbers on their website. Then I talked to some vendors about how they interact with distributors and some warehouse managers about how they deal with inventory."

How to learn about your prospects' day-in-the-life-of

Learning about your prospects' day-in-the-life-of and speaking their language, will enable you to close more sales. While it always helps, you don't have to have experience working in their industry in order for prospects to feel that you *know their business.* Like Ed, you can understand a day-in-the-life-of by learning the following:

- What are the day-to-day challenges? What keeps CEOs, managers, etc. awake at night?
- How will your software affect time, money, personal aggravation, or growth of the business?
- How do they get a raise or get fired? What do they need to do to look and feel good?
- What are the consequences of not achieving their responsibilities? How is their success measured and/or observed?
- What is a day-in-the-life-of now versus when they own your software?
- How will they make smarter business decisions because of your software?

If possible, literally spend time onsite at your customers' place of business for a day (or at least a half day) and observe your customers using your software. Learn what their life was like prior to using the software. Inquire about specifics (dollars, numbers, or percentages) to understand the difference between a day without your software and a day with your software.

When you understand a day-in-the-life-of, prospects will feel that you know their business and that you care about their problems. This understanding develops personal rapport, which predisposes them to purchase software from you.

3. Role in the purchasing process

Amy Swenson's Sales Manager, Ralph Darcy, had a puzzled look when he asked her, "What *exactly* did Slater say that makes you think his Finance Manager has the authority to sign off on the purchase?"

Amy was in a pipeline review meeting with Ralph. They were discussing an opportunity in Amy's pipeline that she had forecast to close at the end of the quarter. Walt Slater was the CFO.

It was due to Ralph's sales coaching skills that Amy had achieved the President's Club award last year. Amy had tremendous respect for Ralph, but sometimes he was direct.

"Well, it *sounded* like..."

"No Amy," Ralph interjected, "not what did it sound like, what *exactly* did he *say*?"

Since Amy couldn't remember the exact words, she had to admit that she drew a conclusion – one that may not reflect reality. Amy and Ralph decided that she needed to reconnect with Walt Slater. She needed him to explain each purchasing team member's role in the purchasing process. Otherwise, she may learn the hard way that the Finance Manager didn't have authority to sign off on the purchase.

It turns out, the Finance Manager had to get approval from Walt Slater before signing a purchase order. And, Walt had to get approval from the CEO!

If you've been in sales for a while, you've probably made the mistake that Amy was about to make. You *assumed* you knew who made the final purchase approval. You found out you were wrong when you lost the sale.

To prevent surprises regarding your prospects' purchasing process, categorize your purchasing team members. Put them in one of the following four role categories.

1. Ultimate decision maker

    This person makes the final decision regarding the purchase of your software. The true *yes* or *no* person. There can be multiple decision makers, like a CEO, CFO, and VP of Customer Service, but typically one person ultimately *owns* the yes/no decision.

    The ultimate decision maker can say *yes* when everyone else says *no*, or *no* when everyone says *yes*.

    The ultimate decision maker tends to need answers to questions like these:

- Does purchasing software make business sense, financially and generally, at this point in time?
- Should this purchase be prioritized now?
- What options were considered?
- How will this software affect customers, investors/shareholders, and employees?

2. Primary contact

This is your *guy* (or gal) who serves as your point person. Sometimes referred to as a coach, this person guides you in the sale and helps you understand the company's software purchasing process.

When your primary contact endorses your software to her peers, she is putting her reputation on the line. If the purchase and implementation go well and business results follow, her reputation grows immensely. Conversely, if the buying or implementation process is rocky, she runs the risk of losing the confidence of her peers.

The primary contact tends to need answers to questions like:

- What is this company's reputation for after-the-sale support?
- Am I providing purchasing team members with what they need to know in order to make a decision whether to buy?
- Can this software implementation be done now?
- How will this software affect my reputation, now and in the future?

3. Approvers

Approvers are all of the other people who will be involved in the prospects' purchasing process.

Approvers can be any of the following:

- Users of the software who will be at the keyboard every day.
- Executives who don't use the software, but pull data for their metrics and dashboards.
- Representatives from legal, financial, human resources, customer service, etc. who don't necessarily receive direct value from your software, but definitely have a say in the purchase decision.

Or some variation of the above!

All approvers can say your software works fine, or not. Some approvers, however, have more decision-making authority than others. For example, someone who is at the keyboard everyday may approve that the software does what it needs to do, but they have no authority regarding the decision: to purchase or not to purchase.

Some approvers may be promotors of your software; others may be detractors. Some detractors may be less influential in the decision process than others. For example, one person may say he does not want your software, but his opinion is easily overruled by other purchasing team members who want your software.

Navigating your prospects' approvers *and* approval authority is crucial. I'll discuss more on that topic later.

Approvers tend to need answers to questions like:

- How will my business day be better because of this software?
- How much of a headache will it be to start using this software?
- Is using this software advantageous to my career?
- How will this software make me, my department, or my boss more effective?

4. Tech dude

This person gives the purchase of your software the Information Technology (IT) okay. If your software meets your prospect's IT team's standards, you get the blessing from the tech dude. Or not.

I distinguish the tech dude from approvers because he sees the software through a different lens. In most instances, he doesn't use the software or get any value from your software's functionality.

Tech dudes tend to need answers to questions like these:

- Will this software introduce any security vulnerabilities?
- What requirements (personnel, technology, compliances, etc.) are necessary for us to support it? Is it in budget?
- Will it integrate smoothly with other applications?
- What are the qualifications of this company's support team members? What is the quality of their support?

If you currently use a role identification methodology, stick with it or determine if a revised approach works better. If these definitions don't match your selling situation, create purchasing team member role categories that are a better match.

Armed with information about purchasing team members' roles in the purchasing process, you will close more sales, faster.

4. Matching features and benefits with titles, responsibilities, and roles in the purchasing process

Importance of knowing responsibilities and roles in the purchasing process

Gustavo Mendez told me that when he started in software sales he was an average producer. Here is how he became a top producer.

Gustavo sells software that manages call centers. Call centers are set up to handle a large volume of telephone calls, especially calls for taking orders and providing customer service.

He was good at understanding various prospects' responsibilities. Gustavo said, "Based on what I learned about my prospects' day-to-day responsibilities and related challenges, I would demonstrate my software to address their needs. However, if I failed to thoroughly understand my prospects' role on the purchasing team, it costs me a lot of sales."

While the specific makeup of a call center varies, in general, call centers have many customers and those customers have many *campaigns*.

A campaign, for example, may be a group of people who man the phones for a customer who runs late night commercials. You know, "But wait. There's more!" When people "call now," the 800 number receives an influx of calls. A call center is at the ready to answer those calls.

Another campaign example is a company that prefers to outsource its customer service department. Rather than hire a team of people to handle phone calls, it retains a call center to deal with the task.

Gustavo's software managed call center staffing, training, call routing, automated attendants (e.g. press one for customer service), scheduling, script writing, problem escalation management, upselling and cross-selling, and more.

Gustavo said, "Each campaign has a manager. I was amazing when showing call center managers how our software made life better. All of them always loved my software!"

He continued, "Sadly, I didn't understand that managers, while being approvers on the purchasing team, didn't have much purchasing authority. They could love my software, but other approvers, like managers' directors, financial team members, and executives were the real decision makers.

Gustavo, now a top producer, said, "Because I can navigate my prospects' purchasing teams' titles and responsibilities *and* understand each person's role and level of decision-making authority in the purchasing process, I'm always on the leaderboard."

Don't be an average producer like Gustavo used to be. Make sure you understand your purchasing team members' level of decision-making authority in addition to their titles and responsibilities.

Matching features and benefits

Based on your knowledge of purchasing team members' titles and responsibilities, and their roles in the purchasing process (including their level of decision-making authority), match your software features and your company's value propositions to their needs.

You will be able to demonstrate relevant features and benefits of your software and discuss your company's overall value proposition for each participant in the decision-making process.

Quick tutorial on features and benefits so we're on the same page.

Every year thousands of drills are sold. But nobody wants a drill.

They want a hole. The drill is the feature. The hole is the benefit.

No one wants anti-lock brakes on their car. They want safety for their family.

No one wants a security alarm system. They want intruder prevention and peace of mind.

No one wants your software. They want what it will do for them. They want *benefits*.

As you demonstrate software, always connect the benefit with the feature. For example:

> *We developed this (feature), so that you will be able to (benefit).*
>
> *In order to make sure you (benefit), we have this (feature).*

Avoid:

> *The software does this (feature).*
>
> *The software does that (feature).*

To clarify and distinguish the features from the benefits, imagine that after every time you demonstrate a feature, your prospect responds by saying, *"So what!"* Be sure to tell prospects *what is in it for them*, the benefits – that's what.

Advantages?

Some sales training programs promote stating the software's features, benefits, and *advantages*. Personally, I feel that approach is more complex than necessary. Benefits and advantages blend.

"You'll love this drill (feature) because it automatically charges (benefit), which means it will always be ready to go (advantage)."

It's your call if you want to distinguish between benefits and advantages.

Features have multiple benefits

Most features have multiple benefits. You do not need to state all of the benefits. Just the relevant ones.

Let's assume a feature of your software is the ability to recognize names based on the phonetic sound, regardless of the spelling. The benefits of this feature include the following:

1. Prevent duplicate entries (e.g. enter *Sedgewick* when it is already in the database as *Sedgwick*)
2. Thwart corrupted databases
3. Avoid contacting the same person twice for the same reason
4. Avoid asking how to spell someone's name
5. Gain rapid access to information
6. Prevent misspelling a name
7. Find a contact when you forget how to spell a name

Based on your pre-demonstration planning, you know that your prospect has challenges correctly spelling clients' names. What sounds like Uhause is spelled Juhasz. What sounds like Rymar is spelled Raymmar.

So, when you demonstrate the phonetic sound feature, you would mention the benefit of preventing misspelled names and not needing to ask how to spell someone's name. It would be great to cover the other five benefits, but time is limited. Focus your software demonstration on the benefits that your prospect needs.

Deciding which benefits and how many benefits to demonstrate is often determined by your experience and instincts, or other words, your art-of-the sale style. It's a delicate balance. Sometimes it is worthwhile to educate prospects about additional benefits of certain features; other times, you are better off only presenting relevant benefits. Consider how a lead was generated, the competitive nature of the opportunity, the time you have to demonstrate your software, and other opportunity specific situations, when deciding which benefits to present.

Take the time to determine beforehand which benefits you want to highlight for the specific prospect.

Make the case for common company features

To sell application software, your company typically has to offer these five features:

1. A user interface (UI) and user experience (UX)
2. Customer support
3. New customer on-boarding
4. Regular software updates
5. Customer user group or conference

If you make a case for the value of a particular *company* feature and your competitor offers a similar feature, but does not make the case for its value, you increase your chances of winning the sale.

Let's make the case for these five common features:

Common features of software	Making the case for the benefits
UI and UX	Because we have team members dedicated to ongoing refinement of our user interface and user experience, we are constantly taking advantage of new technologies and A/B testing to produce the best employee experience. The result: Fewer key strokes required, so employees are more productive. More intuitive processes, which means reduced learning curve for new hires and less need to call support. Software that is easier to use, and even fun to use, which keeps employees happy.
Customer support	Because you are always one click away from access to our customer service team, you will always receive rapid response to your inquiries – it's like having *OnStar* support when navigating our software. We publish the results of our customer satisfaction surveys, which demonstrate that we consistently achieve or exceed our customers' expectations. Our customer service team members are required to pass exams on an ongoing basis to ensure you are always speaking with a knowledgeable expert. We use technology such as incident tracking, call routing, social media, online chat, and screen sharing to enhance your experience with our customer service team. You are always invited to participate in monthly lunch and roundtable discussions with our customer service team, so you have direct access and influence regarding service related issues.

New customer on-boarding	We plan your on-boarding experience in a manner that enables you to do business as usual and not have to work overtime during the process.
	By working backwards from your desired go-live date, we create a plan that is realistic for you and your team.
	We maintain your existing process concurrently until your management team signs off, so you always have a "plan B" should any glitches occur.
Regular software updates	Our software never stops getting better, so you receive regular updates with new features and functionality or improved user interfaces.
	Because we have a rigorous customer needs analysis and consensus gaining process, our software development team can prioritize delivery of the most important, useful new features.
	By using a proprietary development process, our software programmers turn out new releases in record time.
Customer user group or conference	Our customer user group is extraordinarily proactive in the ongoing development of our software, so we consistently deliver what our customers need.
	Whether or not you choose to participate in our customer user group, you still reap the rewards of what it accomplishes.
	Customer user group members tell us they receive benefits beyond just influencing the ongoing development and support of our software. They also build new relationships with other group members and gain industry knowledge they would never otherwise be able to acquire.

I've performed win/loss analysis for clients where customers said the primary reason they bought from my client was because of the software's user interface, the company's user group, or the on-boarding process. However, the competition also had a great user interface, on-boarding process, or user group. The fact that my client's salespeople made a case for the feature became the reason for a purchase decision.

Benefits and negative emotions

Purchasing software can be just as much an emotional decision as it is a financial decision. When a prospect *feels* bad about the status quo because she is not enjoying the benefits of your software, she becomes more motivated to purchase your software. Therefore, it is important to connect the benefits of your software with negative emotions.

Here are some examples:

Benefit	Negative emotion of not having benefit
Prevent duplicate entries	Frustration, aggravation
Thwart corrupted databases	Frustration, embarrassment
Avoid contacting the same person twice for the same reason	Embarrassment, awkwardness
Avoid asking how to spell someone's name	Uncomfortable, embarrassment
Gain rapid access to information	Disillusioned, overwhelmed
Prevent misspelling a name	Frustration, embarrassment
Find a contact when you forget how to spell a name	Frustration, uncomfortable

During your feature/benefit presentations, if you mention the negative emotion associated with not having the benefit, your prospects will see that you are in tune with their real life situations. They will understand the benefit and its personal connection to them and feel that you are a salesperson who *gets* their job.

For example, here is a feature/benefit conversation without mentioning the negative emotion:

> "Phonetic name recognition allows you to find a customer's record using only their name. You type a name as you hear it and all customers whose names sound that way appear on your screen."

Here is the same feature/benefit presentation that includes a mention of the negative emotion:

> "Phonetic name recognition prevents that uncomfortable moment when you have to ask a regular customer how to spell his name. You type the name as you hear it and all customers whose names sound that way appear on your screen."

While the difference is subtle, it is noteworthy to the prospect.

5. Communication styles

I attended two sales calls with Reimund Sudheimer, a top producer who sells software to manage bed capacity at hospitals.

Hospitals with empty beds are similar to restaurants with unused tables, airlines with empty seats, or trucking companies with parked trucks. They don't make money.

Reimund and I met with the Chief Nursing Officer at two different hospitals. Among numerous responsibilities, CNOs are typically responsible for nurse/patient staffing ratios. For example, the Intensive Care Unit may have a target of one or two nurses to one patient, while other departments may target one nurse to seven patients. During the calls, I felt like I was with two different Reimund's. But I wasn't. Here are summaries of meetings with two different CNOs.

Reimund Sudheimer sales call #1	Reimund Sudheimer sales call #2
Reimund opened the meeting, "Hi Susan. Good to see you. I brought reports we discussed on the phone last week."	Reimund opened the meeting, "Great to see you Rebecca. Hey, I tried out Simeone's. Thanks for the recommendation. Natalie said we owe you. How's the new Lexus running? Who gets to drive it to the Cape this summer, you or your husband? I was telling Natalie about your house..."
Reimund showed the CNO the reports and explained how she could manage nurse/patient ratios with the report.	"Using this comparison data, our implementation consultants are able to determine nurse/patient ratios. As you suspected, there are disparities between the OBGYN and the ER. When we compared your statistics to our database of best hospitals, we found you could save in both departments. Can you calculate the cost savings using this comparison data?"

"I plugged in the data that your Director of Nursing provided. Here's the bottom line. You can conservatively save $5M per year."	"Let me explain how your Director of Nursing pulled the data together. Once we enter your data, we run this benchmark report. I'll let you look at it for a minute."
"Next step is to meet with your CFO. Can we coordinate a date now?	"How should we go about the next steps? Would you like some time to digest this information? Do you want to get together with your Director of Nursing to discuss potential next steps?"

When we left sales call #2, I asked Reimund to fill me in on his different sales call approaches to Chief Nursing Officers.

"I've met both of them in person once and I have had a few phone conversations," Reimund said. "Their needs are similar to most CNOs. But their communication styles are so different."

"Go on," I prompted. "How do you know?"

Reimund gave me the *you're kidding, right?* look.

I replied with my hands in the air and a *humor me* look. Reimund told me,

> My first conversation with Susan was on the phone. She was direct and to the point. No small talk. She cut to the chase. The next conversation was at her office. Everything about the office was meticulous. She started by asking how long it took other hospitals we work with to break even on their purchase.

> Rebecca was the opposite. When I met her, she chatted about the weather and her daughter's upcoming prom. Her office was cluttered and her desk was surrounded with family photos.

> Then she switched to high-level hospital strategy before getting into a conversation about our technology.

"And your conclusion?" I asked. He replied,

> Simple. Susan prefers me to get to the bottom line. She has a communication style of, *I don't care about building a clock, I just want to know the time.* Rebecca? Well, her communication style is all about knowing people as people and making sure all T's are crossed and all I's are dotted. I just communicated the way they needed me to communicate with them.

Reimund summed up with his *are you getting this?* look.

How Reimund chooses to communicate with his prospects is the art-of-the-sale. It's about being extraordinarily attentive to the people with whom you speak. The faster you can determine the best communication style to use with each purchasing team member, the easier it will be for you to lead prospects through their buying process.

Reimund did have one more remark worth mentioning. He told me, "If you communicate with everyone the same way, you are not doing your job as a salesperson. You need to be a chameleon. It's the salesperson's job to communicate in the prospect's preferred style... and to be alert for changes in that style over time."

Reimund 's approach was intuitive. He told me he was unfamiliar with formal sales training regarding communication styles, but he had learned the approach in his personal life.

How to identify purchasing team members' communication styles

There are a number of formal approaches to identify and respond appropriately to a purchasing team member's communication style.

An approach many salespeople find useful in understanding how best to communicate is published by *Target Training International* (see ttidisc.com). They use the "DISC" approach to observing human behavior.

> D is for dominance, which is the behavior regarding how people respond to problems and challenges.

> I is for influence, which is the behavior regarding how people influence others to their point of view.

> S is for steadiness, which is the behavior regarding how people respond to the pace of the environment.

> C is for compliance, which is the behavior regarding how people respond to rules and procedures set by others.

All people exhibit all four behavioral factors in varying degrees of intensity. You can observe a purchasing team member's more prevailing behavior and, based on what you observe, you can communicate accordingly.

Here is a breakdown of how to and how not to communicate based on your prospect's DISC observed behavior.

Observed behavior	How to communicate	How not to communicate
Dominance (D) This person is ambitious, forceful, decisive, strong-willed, independent and goal-oriented.	Be clear, specific, brief and to the point. Stick to business. Be prepared with support material in a well-organized "package."	Don't talk about things that aren't relevant to the issue. Don't introduce loopholes or uncertainties. Don't appear disorganized.
Influence (I) This person is magnetic, enthusiastic, friendly, and demonstrative.	Provide a warm and friendly environment. Don't deal with a lot of details (put them in writing). Ask "feeling" questions to draw their opinions or comments.	Don't be curt, cold or tight-lipped. Don't control the conversation. Don't dwell on facts and figures.
Steadiness (S) This person is patient, predictable, reliable, steady, relaxed and modest.	Begin with a personal. comment to break the ice. Present your case softly, non-threateningly. Ask "how?" questions to draw their opinions.	Don't rush headlong into business. Don't domineer or demand. Don't force them to respond quickly to your objectives.
Compliance (C) This person is dependent, neat, conservative, perfectionist, careful and compliant.	Prepare your "case" in advance. Stick to business. Be accurate and realistic.	Don't be giddy, casual, informal, loud. Don't push too hard. Don't be unrealistic with deadlines. Don't be disorganized or messy.

Here's another approach to determining how best to communicate with your purchasing team members. It's similar to DISC, but without the DISC designation.

Behavior exhibited	Characteristics of behavior		How to communicate
Impulsive	Quick Impatient	Hate details Get to the point	Treat with respect, be brief
Deliberate	Very patient Love details	Good listeners Slow decision making	Slow down, be measured
Unsure	Confused by details Not confident	Want your input as to what they should do	Provide reassurance
Self-assured	Authoritative Influential	Talk more than listen Know it all	Stroke ego, move fast
Friendly	Talkative Agreeable	Go on tangents Likeable	Take time to talk about non-business issues
Unresponsive	Indifferent Skeptical	Non-committal Slow in making decisions	Use tact and patience

How to begin identifying communication styles

A simple way to begin learning your prospects' preferred manner of communication is to mirror their style.

Speak in the manner in which your prospect speaks. If they speak fast, speak fast. If they speak about details, speak about details. If they speak casually, speak casually.

If you are meeting in-person, mirror their movements. If they lean back in their chair, lean back in your chair. If they write notes or use a whiteboard, write notes or use a whiteboard.

Try mirroring on your next half a dozen sales calls. You'll find it an easy way to start learning how to identify your prospects' preferred communication styles.

Wrap up on communication styles

Whether you use existing formal approaches to becoming an excellent communicator, or you develop your own hybrid approach, tune in to your prospects. Figure out how best to interact with them. Be like Reimund the top producer, a chameleon, able to navigate sales conversations with purchasing team members by communicating in their preferred style.

Of note, Reimund Sudheimer said that when he first meets any businessperson, he assumes he has precious few *buying* minutes, so he sticks to business and moves relatively quickly through conversations. He said, "I assume my prospect is thinking, *Does this story have an end? Just tell me that part.*"

Reimund said that regardless of different behavioral styles, most business people are under a time constraint. Shortly into a conversation, Reimund is able to *read* new prospects and adjust his communication style to match theirs. He may slow down, provide more details, or discuss non-business rapport building topics. If you have not had the opportunity to learn a prospect's communication style, assume she is a "give me the facts please, just the facts" type of buyer and adjust accordingly as your sales conversation progresses.

There are other approaches to changing your selling approach based on a person's observable characteristics. I find all can be useful. You need to choose an approach that works for you.

How to create a purchasing team profile for your selling situation

Wei Chen is a top producer who sells software to manage large building construction projects.

When asked about his success, Wei said, "Before my demonstrations, I always glance through my purchasing team member profiles. It just takes a few minutes, but it gets me in the zone."

He showed me a few examples of his profiles. They were comprehensive. (See below.) I raised the concern that I suspect many salespeople have. "Wei, this sounds good while we're sitting here talking, but do you really have time to fill out purchasing team profile sheets when you're in the field?"

Wei enlightened me, "It looks like it takes time, but I'm superfast at it. After you have written purchasing team member profiles for a half dozen prospects, it really doesn't take much time."

He also told me that while he conducts his pre-demonstration discovery, he anticipates writing the profile. That helps him keep questions focused in the right areas.

Here is an example of one of Wei's purchasing team member profiles, a Construction Site Engineer.

Responsibilities	Proactively participate in OAC (owner, architect, contractor meetings)
	Write and track RFIs, manage RFI approval process
	Manage field administration with Engineers, Architect, Project Manager, and Supervisor
	Liaise between Project Manager and technical disciplines involved in a project
	Confirm and verify that project is executed per contract
	Manage field operations
	Receive equipment on time and confirm everything is installed on property
	Manage project controls, keep current drawing lists and sets
	Track who'll do what by when on myriad items, like change orders being distributed to the field; keep superintendent informed; organize and implement special scheduling and other day-to-day priorities
Day-in-the-life-of	Pressure to deliver on time and on budget
	Report to numerous people
	Complete or manage mundane matters so focus is on most important projects
	Maintain efficiency
	Carry out or delegate all necessary daily tasks
	Extinguish unexpected fires
	Accomplish observable key performance indicators (KPIs tend to not be measurable)
Role on purchasing team	☐ Ultimate decision maker ☐ Primary contact ☐ Tech dude ☑ User ☐ Other _____
Software features & benefits	Feature: Ability to organize current document sets Benefits:

	Prevent using out-of-date documents, mitigate disputes, save time Feature: Version control tracking Benefits: Keep all subcontractors up-to-date, check for accuracy, easily access historic info Feature: Issue creation and ongoing management Benefits: Track issue resolution time to reward managers Prevent anything from slipping through the cracks Feature: 2D and 3D document saving and file control for rapid access in the field Benefits: Easy access control *Permissioning* of folders for auditing purposes Rapid approval of work flows
Communication style	Slow down, be measured

Creating your purchasing team member profile

Wei uses each of the five elements of a purchasing team member profile (titles and responsibilities, day-in-the-life-of, role on purchasing team, and software features & benefits) that I've discussed above.

Depending on your selling situation, you may want to consider additional purchasing team member profile elements as well. Here a few examples of elements to consider.

Reporting relationships

Use *reporting relationships* (usually identified in an organization chart as who reports to whom) as an element in your purchasing team member profile. When selling enterprise software, decisions are often based as much on internal politics as on solving business challenges.

For example, when selling software to companies that have recently merged, reporting relationships are likely to change. It is important to navigate reporting relationships during your sales process.

Interdepartmental relationships

Use *interdepartmental relationships* as an element in your purchasing team member profile when selling enterprise software where technology alignment is required.

For example, large service-based companies, such as insurers or financial institutions, will need various departmental approvals because software applications will need to be integrated with other software applications.

Best time to call, best way to contact

Use *best time to call, best way to contact* as an element in your purchasing team member profile when decision makers are rarely at their desks.

For example, when selling to construction workers or field service people, you may call at 7am when they're at their desks planning the day, or they may prefer that you use text or email anytime.

Tenure in role

Use *tenure in role* as an element in your purchasing team member profile when purchasing team members with short tenure may not understand their own company's purchasing process.

For example, high growth companies expanding quickly may have many new team members without institutional knowledge.

Software they use or likely use

Use *software they use or likely use* as an element in your purchasing team member profile when making a sale usually requires unseating a competitor.

For example, in a mature market most prospects already own software that performs the task at hand, but they are considering replacing their software with newer and better technology.

Quality of relationship

Use *quality of relationship* as an element in your purchasing team member profile when after-the-sale relationships directly correlate to a successful implementation. A good quality-of-relationship score means prospects are satisfied with your implementation team members and respect their business knowledge.

For example, this relationship is important when customer and software company team members need to have ongoing interaction after the sale.

Personal needs

Use *personal needs* as an element in your purchasing team member profile when the software provides benefits related to individuals, not just the company.

For example, users become certified in xyz software, which becomes a credential on their resume.

What you can do today

- Draft your own purchasing team member profiles based on the five elements, plus any additional elements specific to your sales situation.
- Review your pipeline. Compare what you know about purchasing team members to your purchasing team member profile. Create an action plan based on your assessment.

Chapter 6. How will the purchasing process take place?

Executive summary

• Determine if your prospects have a defined purchasing process by asking purchasing process identification questions.
• Strategies to identify your prospects' purchasing process and how to manage your sales process accordingly.
• When no purchasing process exists, educate about how to purchase software or accelerate the purchasing processes whenever possible.
 	
Chapter details include the following:
 	
   o Examples of purchasing processes that you can model to create an ideal purchasing process for your prospects.
   o Questions to identify your prospects' software purchasing process.
   o Four top producers explain how they manage prospects' purchasing process in order to win sales.

What is your prospect's purchasing process?

Shamus Callaghan, a top producing sales professional, sells software to manage bank teller transactions. While most enterprise banking software programs include a bank teller module, they are woefully inefficient. Because of his company's singular focus on software to manage the bank teller function, Shamus' software has features and functionality that maximizes teller efficiency and prompts Tellers to ask questions and identify sales leads for the Investment Specialists.

Asked about his success, Shamus told me, "Banks purchasing processes vary greatly. Retail banks, commercial banks, online banks and credit unions, all purchase software differently. Even within one bank category, like retail banks, some can make branch level decisions, and others make centralized decisions for all branches. Every bank's purchasing process is unique."

So first on Shamus' pre-demonstration discovery list is, "Please tell me about your purchasing process."

Shamus said that after he gets a general understanding of a bank's purchasing process, he asks detailed questions to understand which people do what and when they do it.

He explained, "There are often purchasing team members who don't even see the software, but they are involved in the purchasing process. For example, Regional Branch Managers rarely attend a software demonstration. Their responsibilities are more strategic. They have nothing to do with the nuances of teller operations. However, they control the budget."

By understanding his prospects' purchasing process, Shamus can lead his prospects through their purchasing process efficiently and effectively.

Purchasing actions

A purchasing process encompasses *concrete* actions that a prospect must take in order to buy your software. What follows are examples of typical purchasing processes for two different software applications.

Note how the software demonstration takes place in the middle of the purchasing process. In order to sell software, your demonstration must be the pinnacle of your sales process, but leading and managing prospects' purchasing activities before and after a demonstration are also of significant importance.

Also note that in all steps the prospect must perform a *concrete action*.

Purchasing process – software for customer self-service on the web

1. Customer complaints lead to recognition of a business problem, which prioritizes a search for finding a resolution.
2. Assess the problem's impact on time, money, personal aggravation, or business growth.
3. Identify team members who should be involved in purchasing process.
4. Determine selection criteria.
5. Identify potential resources to resolve business problems.
6. Assess business case.
7. **Schedule and attend demonstrations.**
8. Observe prototyping (large sales opportunities only).
9. Schedule and attend internal meetings to select solution to problem and *internally sell* team members to acquire self-service software.
10. Check references.
11. Secure legal approval of paperwork.
12. Initiate budget approval process.
13. Create purchase order.
14. Acquire, review, and sign purchase agreement from vendor.
15. Prepare organization for implementation in conjunction with vendor.
16. Begin implementation.

Purchase process – workplace resource management software

1. An event, such as a move or hiring employees, leads to recognition of a business problem, which prioritizes a search for finding a resolution.

2. Establish decision-making process and decision-making team.

3. Outline a plan to find a resolution and assign tasks.

4. Identify options for solving problems via web research and referral requests.

5. Review and narrow down options.

6. **Schedule and attend preliminary demonstrations (executive summary overview).**

7. **Schedule and attend detailed demonstrations.**

8. Play in *sandbox* (an online prototype).

9. Initiate pilot program.

10. Complete return-on-investment analysis.

11. Allocate or reallocate money in the budget.

12. Request corporate authorization to spend.

13. Create proposal with the sales and service team.

14. Satisfy IT requirements.

15. Check references.

16. Secure legal approval.

17. Complete purchasing department process.

Often referred to as the *buyer journey*, I prefer the term purchasing actions.

Journey is defined as, "Traveling from one place to another, usually taking a rather long time; trip" (Merriam-Webster.com)

Action is defined as, "The process or state of acting or of being active"

I'm not into "taking a rather long time!"

Use these examples to create your own list of purchasing actions. Typically, purchasing actions include 6 to 20 steps – all steps involve the prospect doing something concrete. The steps are rarely taken in the same order (some may take place at the same time and be carried out by different people. Some steps may be attended to more promptly, etc.), but it helps to try to list them in the most logical order.

Questions to identify the software purchasing process

Questions	Reason for question
What criteria will you use to make your decision? *How will you determine which software solution is best for your situation?* *Depending on answer:* *How did you decide this is the most important criteria?* *Would you like some assistance creating an evaluation process?*	Identifies the decision-making criteria. Or, identifies there is no decision-making criteria, which puts you in a position to develop a partner relationship and assist with developing decision-making criteria. If you can participate in the creation of a software evaluation process, you can influence the opportunity in your favor.
Have you had to make similar purchases during your tenure with this company?	Identifies whether you will need to lead the purchasing process or let your primary decision maker lead the process.
Please tell me about your software purchasing process. *What are the next steps in your buying process?* *What takes place after you attend a software demonstration?* *Who needs to be involved in those steps?* *At which points in the process will you require approval to proceed and from whom?*	Identifies your prospects purchasing actions. Identifies purchasing team members who may not need to be involved in a demonstration, such as Legal or IT.
Who has responsibility for the financial decision regarding this purchase? *How will you assess your return-on-investment and/or evaluate the business case?* *How will you determine whether this purchase is within your budget?* *Will funds need to be reallocated from other budget items in order to purchase?*	Identifies the status of the cost justification, ROI, or business need justification.

How does that take place? *If you do not create an ROI analysis, why would a senior executive approve this purchase?* *Would you like some help creating an ROI?*	
Will a request for a proposal be created? *Is there a consultant involved?*	Identifies additional steps you may need to take in order to make the sale. You may have to respond to a proposal or you may have to interact with a consultant.
What other options are you considering to solve these problems? What is your familiarity with those options? *Is developing software in-house an option?* *What selection criteria have you established?* *How did you decide these are the most important criteria?* *How will you evaluate software against your selection criteria?* *Do you use any form of rating system to evaluate software?* *Would you like some assistance creating an evaluation process?*	Identifies the competitive nature of the opportunity.

Teach prospects how to purchase software

Marilyn Dayton sells software to manage methadone clinics. Recovering heroin addicts regularly visit methadone clinics. They are administered a dose of liquid methadone in a glass of juice. The methadone inhibits their desire for heroin.

Marilyn's software controls the dispensing of methadone. It also has modules for patient and nurse practitioner scheduling, prescription management, legal compliance, outcome reporting, Medicaid billing, and patient intake and *graduation*.

Few of her prospects have ever purchased business application software.

Most methadone clinics use a mix of spreadsheets, word processing, accounting, and database software. Many of her purchasing team members are social workers who treat patients. Others are nonprofit business administrators, physicians, and grant preparers. Few have much, if any, experience deciding which software is best to manage a business process.

Marilyn said, "I typically teach my prospects how to buy my software. Since my prospects rarely have identified selection criteria or a software evaluation process, I help them do it."

Marilyn provides her prospects with information about how to purchase software, like whitepapers (e.g. an in-depth report on a business challenge that is relevant to your software and how to solve it) and evaluation tools (e.g. a feature checklist to be used after viewing a demonstration).

During her initial conversations, Marilyn learns about her prospects' prior experience purchasing software. She said, "More often than not, they either have never purchased business application software or, if they have, it was not a pleasant experience."

When Marilyn understands her prospects' disposition regarding the purchase of software, she can manage her selling activities appropriately.

"My prospects are always grateful when I teach them about identifying and prioritizing software selection criteria and then creating a process to evaluate software. The best part," Marilyn enthusiastically continued, "is they use *my* selection criteria! And, that's why I achieve my quota every year."

Like Marilyn, Julie Samuelsson is also a top producing sales professional. Julie sells knowledgebase software. Julie said, "Almost all of my prospects haven't been involved in purchasing business application software or, if they have, it's only on one occasion. Part of my job is to teach people how to buy software."

Julie gives her prospects a checklist about what to consider as they assess knowledgebase software. It lists the basics that you'd expect in a knowledgebase, like version control, real-time backup, automatic tagging, and user ratings. But Julie also includes functionality that only her software has, like departmental modules, personal notifications, an executive dashboard, and easy mobile access. Julie say, "Hey, if I'm going to teach them to buy software, it's going to be *my* software!"

Streamline prospects' purchasing process

Once you've identified your prospect's purchasing actions, try to streamline the plan. Work with your prospect and determine the following:

- Can any actions be done in parallel? (e.g. determine selection criteria and initiate an ROI)
- Can the length of time to perform the action be reduced? (e.g. host vendor meetings via phone instead of in-person)
- Can the length of time between actions be reduced? (e.g. schedule dates for preliminary and detailed demonstrations back to back)
- Is the order of the actions efficient? (e.g. have legal review a blank contract earlier in the process)
- Is the buy-cycle action really necessary? (e.g. skip checking references)

- Is there existing information that can make the action easier or faster? (e.g. whitepapers or case studies)

Greg Davis, a top producing sales professional, sells software that enables firefighters to determine water pressure based on a smartphone photo. Greg told me, "Fire departments don't buy much software. In order to purchase software, they have to jump through a lot of hoops. There are budget, timing, and political considerations. I explain that in my position I get to observe how other fire departments go about the purchasing process. Then I make suggestions that keep them moving through the process. They're happy to learn about *best practices* from other fire stations and to shorten the process."

Greg had examples of carving months off purchasing processes by, as he said, "Teaching his prospects how to buy efficiently and effectively."

Greg also said that pipeline review meetings with his manager are quick and simple. "When my sales manager asks, 'How'd the demonstration go?' I tell him, great, they committed to taking their purchasing action tomorrow."

Interdepartmental crossovers

Lisa Keldridge is a top producer who sells software that enables manufacturing companies to move towards environmentally sound practices. Using her eco-concept software, manufacturers can perform a life cycle assessment (LCA) that enables them to design greener products.

Lisa told me about how she botched a sale. (Hey, top producers lose deals too.)

"The prospect was ready to sign. It took me about six months to take out our competitors, work through budget allocation, plan a pilot program, and gain IT approval. We were ready to go!" she exclaimed.

The opportunity was on her list to close that month. Normally, Lisa was an accurate forecaster.

Lisa received a call from Jordan Glass, her primary contact and advocate for her software. "I just heard from Sherry Petersen in the Harmful Materials Department," he said, sounding a little deflated. "She just found out about our plan to purchase your software."

Jordan explained that while his division rarely worked with the Harmful Materials Division, the people in that division were also looking at LCA software designed specifically for harmful materials.

He told Lisa, "Sherry put the brakes on the project until we compare notes. It's going to be important that we have interdepartmental communication on our greener products initiatives."

Lisa said, "I learned the hard way, but now I always inquire about potential interdepartmental crossovers. I sell to global companies. It's actually not uncommon for different divisions or geographic regions to need similar software, but not be aware of each other."

Lisa explained she often identifies other departments that need to be aware of the impending software purchase. "More often than not, my primary contact and I simply have a courtesy call with the department head, who is always grateful. Then we move forward with the demonstration and purchasing process."

Flash forward. Lisa won the sale three months later! The Harmful Materials Department purchased its own software, but they made sure Lisa's software and the harmful materials software could share data.

Top producers proactively inquire about other departments that may have potential involvement in the purchasing process or should at least be made aware of the impending software purchase.

RFPs and consultants

When selling more complex business applications, some prospects retain a consultant to write a request for proposal (RFP) and/or assist with the software selection process.

Responding to RFPs is a topic for another book.

Regarding consultants, treat them as another member of your purchasing team, but recognize that their motivations may be different. Consultants want their clients to install the best software to solve their business challenges, but it is also important that their clients feel the consultant added value and guided them to make the best possible software purchase decision.

What you can do today

- Review your pipeline – determine if you know your prospects' purchasing process.
- If not, find out.
- Once you understand your prospects' purchasing process, lead them through it by asking them to move to the next step(s) of the process

---

Chapter 7. Important pre-demonstration stuff!

Executive summary
<ul><li>Treat your software demonstration as a Hollywood production. Sweat the details in advance of your demonstration.</li><li>Use call recordings and videos of demonstrations to practice, revise, and try again.</li><li>Define *success* before your demonstration, be prepared to sell as a team, prepare an opening slideshow, and don't be Alfred E. Neuman.</li></ul> Chapter details include the following: <ul><li>A variety of top producers discuss their pre-demo planning strategies, including how you can learn from (and avoid) the mistakes they have made.</li><li>The answer to the question, "What if Hollywood produced your software demonstration?"</li><li>Guidance on pre-demonstration activities that set up your demonstration for success.</li></ul>

What if Hollywood produced your software demonstration?

"No, no, no, no," said the frustrated Director, "too much emphasis on the word *kindly*."

The Scriptwriter disagreed. "I think the way he sneers 'kindly' is spot on. I want him to emphasize 'kindly' before he says, 'move over.'"

"You're both wrong," said the Actor. "I don't need to speak here. I can say it with a look. Here, watch."

The Actor gave a disgusted look and gestured with his head.

"That works!" said the Director.

The Screenwriter nodded in agreement.

The Director said, "Okay, let's take a break before we work on the next two lines."

Why don't we put that level of attention to detail into what is being said during software demonstrations?

A friend of mine played an extra in the movie, *The Perfect Storm*. During one scene, my friend was among 50 extras in attendance at the church where the actress Mary Elizabeth Mastrantonio delivered an emotional eulogy.

My friend said that Ms. Mastrantonio had to deliver the same tearful line *seven* times. The Lighting Director kept readjusting the lights to get the perfect shot of Mary Elizabeth and the churchgoers. The Sound Engineer moved the microphone under Mary's shirt because it was picking up her heartbeat during an emotional part, but then the Director decided to move it back because it added to the drama. The Costume Director made the extras seated in the front row change clothing colors because the colors were causing a reflection. During each take, Mary delivered precisely the same lines, cried at precisely the same time, and made precisely the same facial expressions.

Some movie scenes that only take seconds for viewers to watch, take days to film. But those scenes keep you engaged because of the preparation that the director puts into the production process.

Shouldn't sales professionals put that kind of effort into the dialogue, choreography, and screens shown during their demonstrations?

If you approach your software demonstration as if it were produced in Hollywood, you will delight your audience, increase your software demonstration-to-close ratio, and sell lots of *tickets* to your software!

Not a dress rehearsal

Early in my career I sold a manufacturing software application. I was located in the company's Boston branch office. There were about 200 salespeople spread among seven branch offices in our eastern region. Our VP of Sales had the three regional top producers fly to each branch and give a talk about how they achieved their success.

Maria Pulsoni, one of the top producers who had achieved over 200% of her quota, summed up her success with a simple statement, "The demonstration is not a dress rehearsal."

Maria talked about the preparation she did before each demonstration, "I won't even schedule a demonstration unless I know that I can deliver a persuasive and compelling show." She equated presenting a demonstration to performing on stage. Maria was not about to go on stage unless she knew she would receive a standing ovation.

She would meticulously research her prospects to learn about the following aspects of their business:

- Prospect's business challenges and why they are pressing.
- Purchasing team members' roles in the purchasing process and individual needs.
- Buying process and selection criteria.
- The competitive lay of the land.
- Financial situation and how a business case can be made.

Armed with this information, Maria would practice her demonstration. She planned her opening statements. She prioritized which features and functionality she would demonstrate. She planned how she would take out the competition. She anticipated objections and planned how to remove them. She developed the business case. She made sure other people on her own team (e.g. pre-sales engineers, management) understood their roles.

Maria said, "The software demonstration is the defining moment in your sales process. It is the time when prospects decide whether to move forward with their purchasing processes or not. You are on stage – it is not a dress rehearsal. Your audience had better like your act or they won't be buying your software!"

If you want to deliver a successful software demonstration, you are writer, director and lead actor.

Practice, revise, try again

Please be encouraged, not discouraged, by this statement:

> Your software demonstration will never be perfect.

Even if you apply every principle in this book flawlessly, the fine-tuning of your software demonstration is never finished.

Top producers find this exciting. They learn from today's demonstration in order to make tomorrow's demonstration even better.

Top producers practice, revise, and try again. They invest the time to perform a post demonstration debrief (more on this topic later.) During the debriefing, they identify new demonstration concepts to try out during the next demonstration.

This relentless pursuit of improvement is why they are top producers. They outsell their peers and frustrate their competition.

Record your phone calls

Years ago, when I worked in a software sales position that required many hours of phone prospecting, I would record my calls.

During my commute to work, I'd listen to some of the calls.

Sometimes I'd think, *Way to go, Brian!*

Embarrassingly, more often I'd think, *OMG. Did I just say that? Let him finish! Argh, you talked over him. Ask a question about what he just said. You didn't catch what he said about the competition. Brian, that didn't make sense…*

But I learned. My calls never stopped improving. I achieved President's Club recognition every one of the five years I held that position.

Video your software demonstrations

Pick a professional sports team. Any team.

Do you think the coach videos the players? Of course she does.

When pros watch a video of their play with their coach, they are able to hone in on their movements. They can freeze-frame and discuss a swing or a throw. They compare a successful play to an unsuccessful play. They make plans for improvement when they are back on the field.

Have you seen a video of your software demonstration?

Try it. You may not like what you see, but that's exactly why you should video your demo!

Think in sales minutes

Rhonda Petrocelli is a quota overachiever.

"I sell software to busy executives. Until this software purchase thing came up, taking time to sit through software demonstrations was not on their already too long to-do list," Rhonda said with conviction.

"Time is an executive's most precious asset. I don't mess with it."

She clarified, "I'm an executive too, and I manage my time very carefully."

When I asked Rhonda what advice she had for software salespeople who want to sell like she does, she said, "Think in terms of *sales minutes*. There are only so many sales minutes in a day. Use them wisely. Bottom line, my goal is to be preparing for conversations or in conversation with *qualified* prospects every sales minute of my day!"

Imagine how much more you could sell (and how much bigger your commission checks would be!) if you spent the majority of your sales minutes preparing for or actually being in conversation with qualified prospects.

Prepare a pre-opening slideshow

As prospects are entering a room or dialing in to see a demonstration, have a slow rolling three-slide show on display. While attendees are fixing coffee or engaging in pre-demo small talk, they will be viewing key points.

One slide might be a summary of their business challenges. Another slide could be your customers' accolades about your software, and another slide could be a summary of your software's key benefits.

A pre-opening slideshow reinforces your overall sales message and gets prospects curious about what they are going to see during your demo.

Define *success* in advance

A successful demonstration is one where prospects commit to the next purchasing action(s) in their buying process within a timeframe.

If your software demonstration goes well, what will happen next? What will cause you to give your sales manager a thumbs up after the demonstration?

With some software applications, it is feasible to conclude a demonstration and be handed a credit card to charge. More commonly, upon conclusion of a demonstration, prospects need to follow the next steps of their purchasing process (see purchasing actions above).

Don't let, "We need to think about it" be a next step.

Define success *prior* to your demonstration. Have clarity on what those next step purchasing actions will be.

Here are some examples of potential next step purchasing actions:

- Send ROI data by end-of-day Tuesday
- Schedule a demo for the finance team for the week after next
- Send a blank contract today for Legal to start the review process
- Talk to references on Thursday and Friday
- Give the IT guy a copy of the security policy and get feedback by end of week

Note that these examples all include a timeframe. By gaining commitment to a timeframe, you can lead prospects through their purchasing process expeditiously.

Capture prospect data pre-demo

> "An ounce of prevention is worth a pound of cure."
> — Ben Franklin

Time will pass between pre-demonstration discovery activities and your actual demonstration. The less time, the better of course, but delays happen. During that time, you are also working with your pipeline of prospects, many who have similar business challenges. On the day of the demonstration, it is important that you can quickly refresh your memory regarding your demonstration plans.

Develop a method for capturing prospects' important pre-demonstration data in an easy to access format. You need a way of rapidly understanding your prospects' situation so you can tune into their needs and deliver a compelling and persuasive demonstration, without wasting precious sales minutes.

Ideally, use your Customer Relationship Management (CRM) software, but other tools such as Evernote, folder taxonomy and nomenclature, Word, Excel, or a knowledgebase can work just fine.

Enable yourself to easily view a prospect record and immediately understand the following:

- Prospect's business challenges and why they are pressing.
- Purchasing team members' roles in the purchasing process and individual needs.
- Buying process and selection criteria.
- The competitive lay of the land.
- Financial situation and how a business case can be made.

If these bullets seem familiar, it is because they are identical to the ones in the Maria Pulsoni top producer story above!

It's a pain in the derriere to slow down during a sales day and document data, but it's worth the time.

If you spend the time to document the data accurately, you always have what you need at your fingertips. You don't have to ask prospects a question twice. You are more efficient because of easy access to accurate data. While you slow down to enter the data, you speed up everything else.

A pound of cure, as Ben would say.

Team selling

An important part of pre-demonstration planning is to coordinate your selling team's responsibilities.

For example, a sales engineer may be needed to address technical issues, a subject matter expert may be needed to address prospect-specific business challenges, or a senior executive may be needed to influence senior level decision makers.

When team selling is required, the lead salesperson must take responsibility for coordinating the team's responsibilities. Everyone needs to be in lockstep. Each team seller needs to know the following:

- What he or she is responsible for
- When he or she is needed
- What message needs to be communicated
- How the message relates to the other team seller's messages
- What prospects expect from them
- Other relevant items pertaining to the software sales situation

Moreover, an uncoordinated team will raise red flags with prospects, which diminishes its ability to win the sale. When prospects experience a coordinated team selling effort, they feel more comfortable about buying from you!

Don't be Alfred E. Neuman

This really happened. I was observing a demonstration by, for lack of a better alias, Alfred E. Neuman. (Alfred is a cartoon character in *MAD Magazine*. He is goofy. Funny too.)

Seven people were looking at his screen.

A notice popped up on the bottom right, "Yo Dude, you ready for martinis yet? Mary's gonna be there."

Don't be an Alfred. Turn off notifications, close windows, and hide your favorites bar.

Use a screen saver that supports your value proposition. Not recommended: kid pictures, political messages, pets, pregnant wife, drunk friends, and the like.

What you can do today

- Record or video your demonstration. Listen or watch. What works that you should continue doing? What do you need to improve?
- Prepare a pre-opening slideshow that reinforces your overall sales message and gets prospects curious about what they are going to see.

Part Two – Delivering the Software Demonstration

Chapter 8. Demonstration opening

Executive summary
• Captivate your audience with the opening of your software demonstration. Stop them from multitasking, worrying about other priorities, or being distracted in any way.
• Setting expectations up front about your demonstration objectives is a powerful way to get them saying, "Yes," at the conclusion.
Chapter details include the following:
o Examples of *James Bond* openings that you can build on to capture your audiences' attention.
o Tips on how to deliver an opening that sets up your demonstration for success (success also includes a decision to *not* move forward upon conclusion of the demonstration).
o Top producer stories, of course.

James Bond opening

Mary Caldwell is a top producing software sales professional. She sells software to manage the checkout process for counter sales at wholesale distribution companies. Think the contractor counter at Home Depot.

Mary begins her demonstrations with what she calls a *James Bond opening.*

She explains, "The opening of your demonstration should draw in your audience the way a James Bond movie does. Before the opening credits even appear, you are already at the edge of your seat in anticipation of Bond's next action feat."

The enthusiasm in her voice was palpable when she said, "Think about it, Brian. Whether Bond is skiing steep slopes, driving fast cars, or cruising in high speed boats, the audience is asking themselves, 'How's he gonna get out of this one?'"

Mary explained that her opening doesn't get prospects asking *how's he gonna get out of this one*, but they do say, "Wow, this software sounds like something I really need to know about!"

Here's how Mary delivers her *James Bond opening.*

She has two brief role plays.

In the first role play, Sam (one of Mary's peers) plays the role of counterperson. He wears a company cap and blue shirt with his nametag. Bill, (the Sales Engineer) plays the role of the customer. He wears steel-toed shoes, dungarees, and a heavy duty work shirt.

Bill walks up to the *counter* and asks about the availability and price of several plumbing materials. Bill and Sam act out a typical counter transaction with Sam using outdated software with limited features and functionality. Sam fumbles while trying to locate all the materils. Bill displays frustration at the wasted time.

During the second role play Bill and Sam re-enact the same scene using new software. It is a quick, efficient, and pleasant experience. Sam is confident and Bill is relaxed.

After the role play, Mary debriefs the prospect on what the new software had accomplished:

- Bill purchased three additional products because the software prompted Sam with the *customers who bought this, also bought that* feature.
- When a part was not in stock, the software recommended an alternative part. This functionality has the potential to add up to thousands of dollars in additional revenue each month.
- The transaction took 25% less time, which translated into improved customer satisfaction.
- Sam collected cash because the customer was over his credit limit. This situation happens a minimum of 20 times per week in the real world of counter sales to contractors.

In her summation, Mary said, "Based on data from transactions like these, and using sophisticated inventory tracking algorithms, our software will enable three or more inventory turns, *per month* (a key performance indicator for wholesale distributors) compared to the current one inventory turn per month.

That was a James Bond opening. It took less than 10 minutes. I believe the prospect made his decision to buy upon the conclusion of Mary's debrief!

Make sure your software demonstration opening grabs your audience's attention. You need to get busy executives to set aside their thoughts about lengthy to-do lists, the next fire they need to put out, or the upcoming management meeting. You need them to focus and pay attention to you. Engage your prospects. If they aren't engaged, you are selling to a distracted audience. You are prolonging, or worse, losing the sale.

Two more examples of James Bond openings

Example one – gamification software to ensure Occupational Safety & Health Administration (OSHA) compliance.

> At the opening, the audience was invited to participate in a two-minute learning game about shop floor safety. Lights were dimmed while a game-show soundtrack was played.

Participants watched videos clips of shop floor workplaces. Some situations were OSHA compliant. Other situations showed noncompliance issues, ranging from workers with no ear or eye protection and forklifts with no backup warning sound to scarcity of available first aid kits and smoke due to inadequate ventilation.

Participants voted on the degree of OSHA compliance worthiness after each video clip.

When the buzzer went off, a graphical display appeared on the large screen in front of the room.

The salesperson said, "In two minutes everyone just learned about the importance of ear and eye protection, ventilation requirements, and first aid kit locations on the shop floor. What you are seeing on this display is a validation report for OSHA compliance that each of your workers would receive after experiencing a similar video learning session.

He went on to explain how his software would decrease accidents, reduce insurance costs, and mitigate potential for non-compliance, all in less than half the time it currently takes using facilitator-led training.

Example two – software to manage marinas

At the opening, the salesperson said, "I'm going to make a bold statement. Investing in our software will enable you to do the following:

- Complete two to five more boat service orders per *day* (you currently average $475 in profit per service order)
- Maintain slip rental capacity at over 95%, up from today's 80%
- Reduce parts inventory costs while limiting out-of-stock challenges

While speaking, he wrote on a whiteboard: more service orders, increase rental revenue, reduce inventory.

He concluded, "Ready for me to show you how?"

How *not* to start your demonstration

"We specialize in developing websites for nonprofits and foundations. We started in 2002. Since then we have worked with over 250 customers. We are members of the Nonprofit Development Association...," the salesperson droned on in his opening remarks.

Yawn.

Your prospects have seen your website. They know you sell software that they may want to buy. They don't need a dissertation about your company. They need to know how your software will solve their business challenges.

Put the spotlight on your prospects in your opening statements. Open with commentary about your understanding of their business challenges and why they want new software to solve those challenges. Leverage all the pre-demonstration work you've done by showing them that you care, that you spent the time to really understand their business challenges.

Contagious enthusiasm

A mentor of mine (Dave Guarino, Vice President of Sales at Softpoint Data Systems) told me, "After your first interaction with a prospect, you want them to think, 'I *want* what that kid is selling!'"

Dave called it *contagious enthusiasm*. He said, "Imagine me calling you on Thursday evening and saying, 'Brian, I just got two front row tickets to the playoff game tomorrow night. You've *got* to come with me!' Brian, if you said that you didn't want to go to the game, I'd be incredulous. I'd say, '*What*?! What do you mean you don't want to go? Are you crazy?'"

Dave said *that* is being *contagiously enthusiastic*.

Dave said that when he speaks with prospects, he speaks with that type of *contagious enthusiasm*. He said, "When I give a software demonstration, I have an attitude of *I can't believe my prospects would even consider not purchasing my software when they see how it solves their problems!*"

Your opening needs to answer, "So what?"

Mary Connolly is a top producer who sells software to manage tradeshows. Her VP of Marketing was reviewing software that would help the marketing team research and identify new prospects. He asked if Mary would mind sitting in on a few demonstrations, so he could get a salesperson's perspective on the software.

"I was reluctant to sit in on the demonstrations because I have such a busy schedule. I needed to close deals in that quarter. But I couldn't say 'No' to my VP. He's a great guy and he's done plenty of favors for me," Mary said.

She realized that being on the other side of the desk was a great lesson. "It gave me a more in-depth understanding of what it's like to be a prospect."

Going into the demonstration, Mary confessed, "I was thinking, *Really? Why should I care? I've got to get a proposal out today. I have about 15 emails to send. I need to book travel.*"

"That's when a light bulb went off. There is no difference between what I was feeling and what my prospects feel." Mary knew her prospects were always under pressure to plan their next tradeshow. Tradeshow management is complex. The logistics are plentiful, and there are always fires to put out and hard deadlines to meet.

Mary said, "Even though my prospects are considering using my software to improve their tradeshow management process, they feel the pressure of time. Now I always assume that my prospects are thinking, '*So what. Why should I care? I'm busy. My to-do list is overwhelming. Please just tell me how this software works so I can get back to my job.*'"

Mary used her revelation to change her software demonstration opening. Now, Mary acknowledges her prospects' schedules in her opening comments. Then she immediately addresses the *so what* question. She tells them why it is worthwhile for them to break from their busy schedules and invest some time to see her software.

Mary said, "The slight change in my demonstration opening caused a noticeable difference in my prospects' mannerisms. They don't exhibit the *let's get on with it* attitude anymore. They pay attention."

Make sure your opening addresses the *so what* question and your prospects will be more attentive too.

Up front contract

Karina Mirakhur called it her upfront contract. She is a top producing software sales professional. During her demonstration opening, Karina would say:

> I'd like to accomplish three things today.
>
> First, determine if our software is a solution for your business challenges.
>
> Second, discuss the business case; whether investing in our software is cost justified.
>
> And third, determine if our software is the best solution compared to your current situation or any other options in the market.
>
> Only if we get yeses to all three, does it make sense to move forward. Fair enough?

Prospects always agreed that the *agreement* made sense.

Upon conclusion of her demonstration, Karina revisited her upfront contract.

More about that conversation later...

Don't thank them

You can open with either:

> "Thanks so much for your time. I really appreciate being on your schedule..."
>
> or
>
> "You'll be glad you invested the time to learn about our software because you're going to learn..."

Feel the difference?

The first is almost apologetic about taking up the prospects' time.

The second is enthusiastic and communicates that your demonstration is worth every minute of their time.

Contrary to what Mom told us, sometimes you shouldn't say *thank you*.

Agenda setting

Manage prospects' expectations from the beginning.

Here's an opening statement used by a top producing software sales professional:

> Welcome. You'll be delighted that you invested this time to check out our software. I'm so excited to show it to you. Congratulations on your success. Having spoken with all of you, and understanding your prior accomplishments, I'd expect nothing less! We scheduled this demonstration for 45 minutes. Is there anyone who has to leave earlier than 2pm? Today we'll have a conversation about how our software can resolve several of your current business challenges, particularly these:
>
> - Challenge one
> - Challenge two
> - Challenge three
>
> Please ask questions as we go. We'll also discuss why our software is better than other options and justify its cost. If you like what you see, our next steps will be to schedule department demonstrations, enter your data samples, or both. Any questions?
>
> [pause]
>
> I'll start with a brief slideshow to put the demonstration in context. Then I'll take you through the software functionality you'll need to use based on what I learned during our previous conversations.
>
> Does anyone have additions to the agenda?

This opening statement is strong for the following reasons:

- Brevity, preferred by all business people
- Uses *contagious enthusiasm*
- Compliments and congratulates – purchasing team members feel appreciated
- Confirms the time (if someone has to leave early, you can cover software relevant to them first or schedule to meet individually)
- Reiterates why life today is not so good, which creates interest in seeing the software and learning about a better tomorrow
- Invites conversation
- Introduces competitive comparisons – letting them know this is a topic you feel comfortable in discussing
- Tells them that the business case or ROI will be addressed
- Acknowledges potential additions to the agenda

During introductions, sell your teams' bios

Tout your team members' bios! They create credibility for your company.

Your company has employees who have achieved notable degrees, received awards, written industry publications, or spoken at conferences. Leverage these accomplishments as a competitive advantage.

Get your marketing team involved in creating bio *talking points*.

Here is how a top producing software salesperson introduces his sales engineer and implementation specialist to his prospect's CEO:

> Bill, I'd like you to meet Joe and Mary.
>
> Joe is our sales engineer. Joe holds dual degrees in software engineering and computer science. Before joining our company five years ago, Joe worked in your industry, so he's intimately familiar with your business challenges. He is responsible for ensuring you have no problems with technology integration.
>
> Mary is our implementation specialist. She has been making sure software implementations are flawless for two years now. She's just back from being a guest speaker at the International Software Implementation and Support Conference in Vegas.

These introductions share these characteristics:

- Brief
- Sold the sales engineer's and implementation specialist's qualifications
- Provided clarity on who does what
- Use your introductions to set the stage for a successful demonstration. You want your prospects thinking, *Wow, this team is impressive!*

Here is how he introduces the CEO to Joe and Mary: "Joe and Mary, I'd like to introduce you to Bill Jones. As CEO of NetSoft, Bill is the reason the company has grown 40% per year for the last three years. Bill was recently quoted in the *Tech Times* news about..."

This introduction accomplished the following:

- Complimentary to the CEOs track record
- Demonstrated that the salesperson did his research on the CEO (e.g., *Tech Times* quote)
- Reminded Joe and Mary with whom they would be speaking

Positioning to solve business problems

Once you have your prospect's full attention (because you delivered a creative opening), review with your prospect three to four of her most pressing challenges, which you learned during your pre-demonstration discovery. At this point, you should be able to summarize in about five minutes what you have learned about the effects those challenges are having on time, money, personal satisfaction or business growth.

This discussion raises expectations that the demonstration will deliver an opportunity to see and learn about a product that will be highly relevant and deliver real value to the company. It also gives participants an occasion to prioritize what they want the software to accomplish and a chance to confirm or further discuss challenges that the software can address.

Finally, the discussion distinguishes you as a sales professional who both cares about and understands your prospect's needs. You've done your homework. Now you are positioned to connect the features and benefits of your software to solving the prospect's challenges (her reality), and to highlight the negative consequences of staying with the status quo.

Start time

I realize why it's done, but I still get a kick out of it. My doctor's office tells me to show up 15 minutes early for my 2:00 pm appointment.

I think, "Why not just tell me we have a 1:45 pm appointment?" I know the reason is to make sure the doctor doesn't have down time due to late patients. When a doctor isn't seeing patients, she is not billing.

If you show up on time for a meeting, but have to wait for the meeting to start because someone else shows up late, it doesn't feel right. Because it isn't right.

A best practice is to start your demonstrations on time, maybe wait a few minutes if the CEO is running late, but no more. Those who arrive on time will be appreciative.

For the latecomers, acknowledge their arrival. Let them know you'll schedule an individual conversation to catch them up.

Arrive early

It's so frustrating and it happens so often. Technical difficulty causes a delayed start of your demonstration. Prospects have security issues, projector's bulbs burn out, dial-in numbers don't work, audio or video won't play, etc.

To mitigate the tech delay, always arrive early for your demonstrations. If you are delivering a web demo, dial in ten minutes early. For in-person demonstrations, depending on the complexity, arrive 15 to 30 minutes early to set up and test your equipment.

Value of small talk prior to demo

Online or in-person, the small talk that takes place while the purchasing team is assembling for the demonstration presents an opportunity to sell. Make your small talk relevant.

Rather than discussing the weather, the ballgame, the kids, or the traffic, focus the conversation indirectly on the sale and the prospect. Chat about a satisfied customer with similar challenges; your prospect's involvement in an industry association, which you noticed on his LinkedIn profile; industry trends; or perhaps ask a few confirming questions.

Managed thoughtfully, these small conversations advance the sales process and distinguish you from your competitors. The purchasing team is attending the demonstration in order to make an extremely important decision, not to hear about last night's ballgame or the weather.

As mentioned earlier, keep the spotlight on your prospects. Your demonstration is all about them from the opening minute to the closing minute.

Build rapport with commonality

Commonality builds rapport.

We meet for the first time at a business networking event. I saw you drive into the parking lot in your Jeep. I own a Jeep. We instantly connect and discuss our thoughts on Jeeps.

It could be getting a parking ticket, coming from the same state, common connections on LinkedIn, wearing the same sweater, having five-year-olds, attending the same school, knowing the same person… you get the idea.

Find something in common with your prospects. It will build rapport, and once you build rapport you have more productive sales conversations.

Use names

Dale Carnegie in *How to Win Friends and Influence People*, one of the greatest sales books not written about sales, says, "People love to hear their name. So use it."

Take a lesson from Dale, remember to refer to purchasing team members by name during your opening remarks and throughout your demonstration.

Compliments

People like compliments. Compliments make you feel good when you give them, make the recipient feel good to receive them, and take seconds to give. Why not compliment people?

Compliment your prospects on their success throughout your demonstrations. Mention how they do things better than similar companies you have worked with, without mentioning company names, of course. Mention individuals' accomplishments. Be a fan of their success!

A note of caution. Your compliments must be sincere or you will sound *salesy* and diminish your credibility.

What you can do today

- Fine-tune your demonstration opening statements and introductions to ensure prospects are engaged.
- During your next three demonstrations, agree about the conclusion of the demonstration at the beginning. If your demonstration is successful (or not), how will you decide? What criteria will enable your prospect to move forward with the purchasing process?
- Evaluate findings. Change your sales process accordingly.

Chapter 9. Five elements of a winning software demonstration

Executive summary

An unparalleled software demonstration has all of the following characteristics:

1. Engages all purchasing team members
2. Presents in a memorable manner
3. Explains how your software solves pressing business challenges
4. Justifies the cost
5. Outperforms any other options

Chapter details include the following:

- o Step-by-step guidance on how to master each of the five elements of an unparalleled software demonstration.
- o Ways to avoid the most common software demonstration mistake – teaching prospects how the software works instead of persuading prospects to purchase it.

An unparalleled software demonstration

Based on my experiences observing hundreds of demonstrations and interviewing countless top producing software sales professionals, here is my definition of an unparalleled software demonstration:

> *An unparalleled software demonstration is one in which you present to all purchasing team members, in a memorable manner, how your software solves their pressing business challenges, justifies the cost, and outperforms any other options.*

Let's break this definition into its five important elements:

1. To all purchasing team members who have some influence in the buy decision.
2. In a manner that makes a favorable impression – one that will be remembered.
3. How your software solves their pressing business challenges.
4. Why your software is cost justified (demonstrates the ROI using their business data).
5. Why your software outperforms any other options (is demonstrably better than the competition).

Let's dive into the details!

1. Demonstrate to all qualified purchasing team members

Herding cats

In the pre-demonstration discovery chapter, I discussed strategies for identifying purchasing team members. The next challenge is persuading those purchasing team members to attend your demonstration.

Have you ever tried to get just one cat to respond to your commands, requests, or pleas? She'll take a message and get back to you.

Sometimes you'll feel like you're herding cats when you are trying to coordinate a software demonstration with multiple purchasing team members.

It's a sales process in and of itself to persuade purchasing team members that it is in their best interest to all attend a demonstration together.

When all purchasing team members attend demonstrations as a group, you and your prospects benefit. Here's why:

- Everyone's questions are answered and heard by all purchasing team members, which keeps purchasing team members on the same page. It often spurs important conversations about how the software will work at their company. Any conflicting needs between purchasing team members are identified.
- When prospects see features and functionality together, instant consensus as to the software's value can be gained.
- It saves time – it doesn't take as long for purchasing team members to reach a yes or no decision.
- Information is fresh in your prospects' minds during internal debrief sessions afterwards.
- After-the-sale surprises or problems are mitigated for both the buyer and the seller because when everyone is in the room, everyone is on the *same page*.

Sell your prospects on attending your software demonstration as a team. Unless you are demonstrating software that is used by the entire enterprise (many teams with different needs), like Tonya Edwards.

When demonstrating enterprise software

Tonya Edwards sells six-figure software to manage the middle-to-back office needs of global investment firms. She went from being an average performer to a top producer. She told me how:

> When I started working here, I followed the same sales process as my peers. I scheduled a day on site at my prospect's business where, along with my sales engineer, we demonstrated our software to everyone who would use it.
>
> Inevitably we'd be showing software modules to a few people who were interested and excited while others in the room would zone out and check their smart phones.

Her software had modules for corporate action processing; internal, client and regulatory reporting; performance measurement and attribution; and post trade compliance.

Tonya told me that because her software was an enterprise solution and involved so many departments, many users of the software were also purchasing team members. They would need details regarding their department's use of the software.

Tonya said, "I broke the full demo day into 45 minute sessions customized for each of several select departments, so I could focus on solving their business challenges. There were no more people checking smart phones!"

It took Tonya some trial and error to plan her ideal demonstration schedule. For example, the post-trade-compliance team tended to need more than 45 minutes. Also, it usually worked best to combine the regulatory reporting team with the corporate-action-processing teams because the software modules were intertwined.

Here we are at the art-of-the-sale again. Ideally, all purchasing team members should attend your demonstration at the same time. However, there are exceptions, such as Tonya's.

Top producers constantly refine their approach to software demonstration scheduling. There are only so many sales minutes in a day. If you can sell your software in two demonstrations instead of four, you've shortened the time to a sale and to your commission check.

Worst case

Okay, you've tried everything to persuade the purchasing team members to attend the demonstration at the same time. But your efforts didn't work. You will have to schedule a second demonstration with different purchasing team members.

- Before the demonstration, gain clarity from your primary contact regarding next steps. Learn what needs to be accomplished in demonstration one in order to get a green light on demonstration two.
- Before agreeing to the date for demonstration one, make sure the rest of the purchasing team is available in the near future to attend demonstration two. Long gaps between demonstrations makes gaining consensus on a purchase decision more difficult.
- As you progress through demonstration one, ask the purchasing team members which modules you should feature during demonstration two.

Upon conclusion of demonstration one, you should have a clear understanding as to what the constituents attending demonstration two will need to see.

Use scheduling software

A client of mine sells software to educational institutions – colleges mostly. Sales team members were spending an average of four hours per week scheduling their next week's travel. Emails or phone calls back and forth sounded like this:

Prospect: "Okay, next Tuesday the 7th at 11am works for Professor Scott and Professor Hunt. We haven't heard from Professor Jameson yet."

Salesperson: "Great, thanks. But I'm meeting with Adam Lalina, the Treasurer's assistant at the library at 1:30pm. I'll need 40 minutes to get to the other campus where the library is."

Prospect: "We'd have to meet at 10:30am then, but I know Professor Scott can't make 10:30am. How about the week of the 25th?"

Imagine four hours of that every week.

Using appointment scheduling software, the team was able to reduce this four-hour headache to 15 minutes. The salesperson simply shared his calendar with open dates and times to meet. The purchasing team did the rest.

There was an added benefit. One of the sales team members, who trialed the scheduling software said, "There's a guilt factor that takes place. Professors tend to clear their schedule when they see their peers have accepted a particular day and time. They don't want to be the one person who messes things up."

If you are scheduling multiple purchasing team members, consider purchasing appointment scheduling software.

How to stop no shows

It is disappointing when you have a software demonstration scheduled and the prospect doesn't show up. It is definitely worse if it's an in-person demonstration, particularly if you've traveled far in order to deliver the demonstration. For web demos it's not as bad, but it still plays havoc with your day and wastes your sales minutes!

You can run the numbers on your no-show statistics. For example, you close four out of ten demonstrations. Your no-show rate is five in ten; that's fifty percent of scheduled demonstrations not happening! What's the value of acquiring a new customer? If your no-show rate dropped to two in ten, how would that impact revenue? When you plug in the numbers, reducing demonstration no-shows is a low cost, high return initiative worth prioritizing today.

Everything is a sale. You have to *sell* prospects on the importance of attending or notifying in advance if they cannot attend.

Depending on your sales organization structure, Marketing may be responsible for scheduling demonstrations. Whoever does it, here are several ideas to mitigate no shows:

Email in advance

Send a confirmation email with an invitation to reschedule three days in advance.

Send a confirmation email the afternoon before or morning of the demonstration.

Call in advance

Leave a confirmation voicemail.

If you connect, have a confirmation call script.

Whether you make calls or send emails, be prepared with a benefit statement. Why is it worth their time to attend your demonstration?

When scheduling

Offer times on the 15s or 45s. For example, when discussing a date for a demonstration, you may ask, "Can you be available for a demonstration at 2:15pm on Wednesday? Otherwise, on Thursday I'm available at 9:45am or any time after 3:00pm."

Prospects tend to show up on time when a meeting is scheduled for a 15 or 45.

(More on this later in the *busy restaurant* section.)

Worst case

No matter how well you use email and phone calls to prevent no shows, sometimes prospects don't show up. This *worst case* isn't so bad. Prospects feel guilty when they don't show up or cancel at the last minute. Now, you can use it against them!

"I'm so sorry you couldn't make the last demonstration…"

Message delivered and received.

One top producer told me he thinks of no shows like this, "If they can't make the demonstration it is all the more reason they need my software. They obviously have a challenge managing their time, which my software can fix."

Use email, voicemail, and conversation planning to mitigate your no shows.

2. Demonstrate in a memorable manner

Why demonstrating in a memorable manner is important

A conversation between three purchasing team members while discussing the pros and cons of software demonstrations they had attended over the last month:

Manny, VP Operations said, "Bill, it was TriPoint that had the auto-upload ability, not TitleWave Systems."

"I'm telling you, it was TitleWave," Bill, IT Director, replied adamantly.

"Hold on guys, take a coffee break or something and let me take a look at their websites," Kristy said. She was the Regional Administrator and often the mediator for these dust ups.

Bill said, "Thanks Kristy, you rock. While you're at it, can you confirm that TitleWave was the one that had benchmark data built into the inventory cost reports?"

Kristy replied, "Bill, they do, but they charge for it, remember?"

"By the way, didn't that guy from 11Point3 Software say they were going to have benchmark data in the next release?" Manny asked.

"It's *3Point11,* Manny, and no, he said benchmark data was on the development roadmap. We're not buying vaporware." Besides, Bill said, "It's more important that we get the 24/7 support that TelVolt offers because all four of the software packages get the basic job done."

Put yourself in the prospects' position. They're busy. They're working hard. They know there may be a better way of doing things, but they have seen numerous salespeople all selling similar solutions. They must take time away from an already hectic schedule doing business (aka, making money) to take a look at software that is supposed to be able to help.

Most software will appear to deliver a better way of doing business than the software they are currently using. Screens flash before their eyes while someone who claims to understand their business demonstrates all kinds of features and functionality.

Days or weeks after seeing demonstrations, the purchasing team meets to consider its options. Frequently software demonstrations blend together. It's a problem to remember which software had what features.

Avoiding the confusion abyss is why your software demonstration must be memorable. You need your prospects to remember what they see and why it is important to them!

When you deliver a memorable demonstration, the Mannys, Bills, and Kristys of the world will not be having the above conversation about your software.

Here are ways to make your demonstration memorable.

Drive home a couple of key points

Telly Monteith, a top producer who sells software to manage large accounting firms, told me, "I drive home two key points all the way through my demo and in my follow-up emails. I make it easy for purchasing team members to remember why our software is the best."

During the opening of his demonstration, Telly told his prospects,

> Our support technicians are former Certified Public Accountants who all worked at large accounting firms, so your software implementation will be flawless and the people you speak with on our support team will know how to assist you.

> We only sell to accounting firms that have high tech manufacturers or biotech companies for clients, so our software is designed around your client's accounting requirements.

Telly explained that he drives home these two points throughout his demonstration. He uses statements like these:

> That's why you want CPAs designing your software.

> If you had that question in real life, you'd make one call and your support technician would give you the answer.

> Since this compliance issue is only required by biotech firms, we built this safeguard into the software.

> Your high tech clients will love this feature for tracking the cost of hazardous chemicals!

Telly said, "Ask my prospects about our software a month later, and they'll say, 'That's the company that has CPAs doing support. They only work with accounting firms that have tech company clients.'"

Restating and demonstrating the importance of a few key points throughout the demonstration will ensure your prospect remembers important competitive advantages. Pick two to four key points – no more – that you want to drive home in your demonstration and continually refer back to them.

Here are some generic examples of key phrases to give you some ideas:

- Strength of intelligent user interface design
- Unparalleled implementation process
- Accurate one-time data entry
- Unprecedented data conversion speed

Make in-person demos an experience

Make in-person demonstrations an *experience* for your prospects!

- Post a welcome sign.
- Meet prospects immediately upon arrival.
- Make sure the office is organized and spotless.
- Serve *really* good food with healthy (and not-so-healthy) options.
- Prepare personalized information packets.
- Give prospects a relevant promotional product (something nice like a desk clock, a puzzle, or golf balls).
- Be sure that anyone who will be meeting your prospect is prepared with a warm welcome.
- Arrange transportation (limo) if prospects are flying in.
- And anything else you can think of that will distinguish your company and employees and deliver a memorable experience!

I once met a sales pro who sold six-figure software. He went above and beyond to deliver an experience. He arranged to fly three purchasing team members to a site visit with an existing client on a chartered jet. *That* was an experience.

Enter prospect's data in advance

When prospects see their customers' names, their vendors' names, their parts numbers, their sales team members' names, their projects, or anything that is *theirs*, your demonstration becomes more memorable.

Enter prospects' data in advance of your demonstration.

Tell, tell, tell

If only we could tell somebody something once and know they had heard and retained what we said. CEOs could give a speech on the company's direction once a year and the company would be super profitable. Students would attend a class and get an A on the next day's test. It would be like reading this book and instantly being able to use every strategy tomorrow.

Your prospects need to hear about your software's value proposition multiple times, in multiple ways.

During your demonstrations, tell your prospects what you are about to tell them, tell them, and then tell them what you just told them.

It's called the tell, tell, tell strategy.

"Telly" (mentioned above) applied the tell, tell, tell strategy flawlessly.

Use memorable statements

You have bragging rights that your company or software has earned. Use them to create memorable statements to salt throughout your demonstration. Try one of these examples:

> *We've been working in this industry for over 15 years.*
>
> *More than 85% of our customers converted from competing systems.*
>
> *The majority of the top firms in the industry use our software.*

Cite statistics and benchmark data

A statistic is a quantitative fact or statement. Statistics *stick* in your prospects' minds. Businesspeople are always interested in statistics. They want to know how they stack up against similar companies or other execs who have similar responsibilities.

Here are some examples:

> *In a study of 100 CEOs, the Hillcrest Research Group found that more than 63% were planning to invest in software because…*
>
> *Last year alone, Selltone Research found that companies using software to… increased profit margins by an average of 12%.*
>
> *Less than 10% of all… [retailers, distributors, etc.] are prepared for the new… laws coming into effect on March 15th.*

Statistics and benchmark data drive home key points. Because they are from reputable sources and because they always reference dollars, numbers, or percentages, they are very memorable.

Give control of the mouse

Nick Petrove sells software to manage printing presses. He is a top producer. Nick said, "I give prospects control of the mouse three times during my demonstrations. They love it."

Nick explained that he poses a challenge during the demonstration. I tell them, "When you log on in the morning, this dashboard flashes red." Then I click the dashboard and ask, "Now what do you do?" I give control of the mouse to a purchasing team member. The software is intuitive. Prospects always click around while I tell them how they can use the dashboard data to make smart decisions.

Nick said, "While they're playing with dashboard, I discuss common concerns of print-press software purchasing team members, such as ink usage, number of print pages per hour, meantime-between-failure, paper options, technician support, mail delivery, and a lot of other matters that lets prospects know that I understand their day-in-the-life-of.

Nick involved his prospects by giving them control of the mouse. His prospects *saw* with their eyes, *heard* with their ears, and *felt* with their hand on the mouse as they made things happen within the application. The prospects had hands-on experience, so they remembered the software.

Nick smiled, "They don't forget my demos!"

Get them talking about how they'd use the software

Matthew Alterzen is a top producer who sells software for security guard management.

During his demonstrations, Matt tells his purchasing team members, "I've entered three incidents that recently occurred here into the software. I'll let you tell me how you'd use the software."

This prospect was a security guard company that serviced residential condominiums. Matt had entered these incidents: a broken window, a resident noise violation, and a water leak.

While Matt demonstrated how the software can assist, an ensuing conversation led to discussion regarding which incident to prioritize, which people guards need to notify, and what information the property management team will need to tell its residents.

Matt said, "When I get them talking about how they'd use the software, they never forget it."

Use analogies or metaphors

Prospects remember analogies and metaphors because they evoke experiences. It is the difference between *seeing* an ice cold ocean and *being in* an ice cold ocean. All of your senses are intensified when you are in the ocean. (How did that analogy work on you?)

Dictionary.com definition of Analogy:

   A similarity between like features of two things, on which a comparison may be based.

Example: *Using our software is like driving in the Indy 500 instead of a go-kart race.*

Dictionary.com definition of Metaphor:

   A figure of speech in which a term or phrase is applied to something to which it is not literally applicable in order to suggest a resemblance.

Example: *Remember using Etch-a-Sketch when you were a kid? You picked it up and started drawing. This report generation screen is an Etch-a-Sketch x 1000.*

Turn on your camera

If you are demonstrating via a web conference, click your camera on so that prospective customers can see you giving the demonstration. Your prospect's experience improves immediately. There's the added visual interest of your facial expressions in addition to what's happening on the computer screen.

If your competitor doesn't turn on his camera, and you do, you gain a competitive advantage. People like to buy from people. When they can look you in the eye and see your facial features as you speak, you transition from a voice on the phone to a person in the flesh. You humanize your software demonstration.

Let your competition be a disembodied voice on the phone while you're the *person* whom they can hear and see.

Give consideration to the lighting, the background, and your appearance.

Adjust the lighting so people can see you best. Lighting that's too bright or too dim, or causes a reflection from eyeglasses or a picture frame can be distracting.

Carefully consider your background. A bookshelf with industry-related books behind you looks better than a cubicle wall with notes pinned on it. The bookshelf shows prospects that you are someone who stays on top of industry issues.

If you have a tradeshow booth, consider using it as your background. The marketing message is sure to support your software's value proposition.

Pay attention to your appearance as well. History teaches us a valuable lesson about on-camera appearance. In 1960, viewers saw the first televised presidential debate between Richard Nixon and John F. Kennedy. Polls after the debate showed that people preferred JFK. Nixon needed a shave and was sweating. Kennedy made sure he had a deep tan for the televised debate. Nixon looked shifty while Kennedy looked healthy and confident. So don't be Nixon; be JFK and make sure you look your best.

Use humor

If you smile and laugh, you are enjoying yourself. Get prospects to smile and laugh and they'll enjoy themselves as well.

Show a Doonesbury cartoon, tell a humorous story, or be self-deprecating.

Or, tell a joke... with this caveat. It must be well-practiced, short, appropriate, relevant, inoffensive and proven to be funny.

One salesperson who started turning his camera on for web conference demos used it as a humor moment. When prospects were first logging in and they'd see him on camera, he'd comment, "You can see me, but I can't see you." He said, "People thought for a moment and chuckled. I think they were imagining what it would be like if I could see them."

Ooh, ah features

Business application software will often have what I call *ooh, ah* features. This functionality always causes prospects to lean in with interest and say, "Cool!" (Or *ooh, ah!*)

For example, a big data application that sorts through more than one billion data points and instantly provides a graphical image of the results with one mouse click.

Or an HR application that parses candidates' resumes, categorizes skills and experience, matches candidates to open positions, and immediately delivers interview questions for hiring managers.

Or a biotech application that cuts testing procedures from two months to two days using multivariate testing.

Whether the features are entirely relevant to a particular prospect or not, if the prospect has an *ooh-ah* response when told about them, consider demonstrating them to make your demo more memorable.

Use customer testimonial videos

Show a video clip of happy customers endorsing your software.

It's so easy to do, yet so few software companies do it. Ask your customers to give you a video testimonial. Most are delighted to help.

Salespeople, marketing and customer service reps, and anyone else who meets with customers in-person need to be equipped with a video camera and a mission to get a testimonial. The equipment is readily available today via the smart phones we all carry.

Using a coordinated game plan, you can compile an ongoing stream of compelling customer testimonial videos to use in your software demonstrations. The next ten in-person customer meetings should yield at least five customer testimonial videos.

Simply ask your customers to give you a brief statement about why they purchased your software and how it has worked out. Then turn the camera on.

A little editing by your Marketing team and your memorable video of customer testimonials will be good to go!

Note: some of my clients find it easier to distribute cameras to the folks who will be shooting the testimonials. Then all videos are stored on a camera that can be *turned in* after a video shoot. It's faster and easier than asking salespeople to email their video clips after shooting them, and it's easier for the marketing team to manage, edit, and publish incoming videos.

Use written customer testimonials

Written testimonials are also memorable.

Start by simply asking your customers for them. The response is almost always favorable. People like to help people.

However, customers frequently have other priorities that push writing a testimonial to the bottom of their to-do lists.

Make it easy for your customers to provide testimonials. Send a draft of the type of testimonial you'd like to receive. Give them the opportunity to edit the draft (they almost never do). Appreciative that you saved them time and got it off their to-do list, they most often sign off on it!

For example:

> "We decided to go with ABC Company after an exhaustive search. None of the other companies we talked to was able to customize a program for our needs. In the first three months of the program, we saw a 20% increase in sales in our two main product lines. The support has been stellar. When we have questions, we get instant answers and the follow up has been consistent and professional."
>
> Mary Jones, VP Sales, Westwood Technology Corp.

This is a long form testimonial. It is best for use on your company's website or in proposals. For use in your software demonstration slideshow, convert it to short form so it is easier for purchasing team members to glance at and understand the endorsement.

Here is a short form version of the same testimonial:

> "...20% increase in sales in our two main product lines. The support has been stellar... instant answers ... consistent and professional."
>
> Mary Jones, VP Sales, Westwood Technology Corp.

Here's another long and short form version of a customer testimonial:

> "We've worked with other web promotion companies, but none was able to drive the high volume of referrals we saw from our ABC Company program. In our first quarter, we saw over 200 referrals and more than a 4.3X return on investment on the e-mail referrals alone."
>
> Dr. Bill Smith – Owner, Bayview Clinic

"... high volume of referrals from ABC... over 200... 4.3X return on investment."

Dr. Bill Smith – Owner, Bayview Clinic

Note that both short and long versions include measurable results and a statement about why the prospect chose to use your software.

Use customer testimonials during the slideshow portion of your demonstration or on the opening slide when your meeting is convening. Testimonials make your demonstrations memorable!

The more endorsements the better

Please, play the role of a hiring manager for a moment.

You have interviewed two salespeople, both of whom you like, and both of whom have relevant experience and evidence that they can do the job. But, you only have an open requisition for *one* additional salesperson.

While you are pondering your decision, both candidates proactively send you their reference lists (not surprising coming from top producers).

Candidate A sends you three names, a former sales manager, a coworker, a human resources person. Candidate B sends you seven names, two customers, four former sales managers, and two CEOs.

What is your perception? Doesn't Candidate B already seem like he'll be your choice? It's easy to think that since so many people will attest to his sales talents, he must be good.

And you didn't even talk to the references yet! References are endorsements. They are testimonials to a candidate's qualifications.

As in hiring, references also apply in software sales – endorsements matter.

Another example: You view someone's LinkedIn profile. In the top skills section, you see that she has a half dozen skills listed with "99+." That means over 100 of her colleagues have endorsed her for those skills. What is your perception? Once again, she must be good.

When you have a long list of customer endorsements, or existing customers willing to take a reference check call, prospects will have the perception that your software must be better than competitors who have fewer endorsements.

New and useful information

Picture your prospect reading her email the morning after your demonstration. Would it increase the memorability of your software demonstration if she had a follow-up email from you that included new and useful information?

Send additional *new and useful* information immediately post demonstration.

Use snail mail

Send something (e.g. a thank you note, promotional product, or whitepaper) via snail mail. It's doubtful that your competitors will, so it distinguishes your company and makes your software memorable. It's fun to receive snail mail that isn't junk mail!

What you can do today

1. Identify ways to make your demonstration even more memorable.
2. Deliver a demonstration or two.
3. Regroup and assess what worked and how you can make your demo even more memorable.

---

3. Demonstrate how your software solves pressing business challenges

How a higher cost competitor's demonstration won deals

Early in my career, I sold software to manage the process of pharmacy prescription fulfilment. I worked for SoftPoint Data Systems, a Long Island, NY, based company.

These were the days when mom and pop pharmacies still thrived. Software to manage pharmacies was a new concept.

Everywhere I turned, prospects would tell me, "No thanks, I bought a system from Tom Modeen." Tom worked at Script Systems, a primary competitor.

The Script Systems solution cost more ($30k vs. $20k for the SoftPoint solution) even though it offered similar features and benefits.

Realizing I couldn't beat Tom, I persuaded Joanne Guarino, CEO of SoftPoint, to hire him. (Hey, got any better ideas?)

With Tom on the team, I learned his secret to winning deals from competitors whose software was less expensive. It was the effectiveness of his software demonstration. Tom showed prospects how the software would solve pressing business challenges.

When I demonstrated the software, I sounded like this:

"Here's how easy it is to enter a new patient's name. You can spell Rodriguez multiple ways and find the patient. These are the drop downs where you select an insurance plan with an automatically validated number. You can pull up patients' invoices on this screen. This is a list of all the reports the system can generate..." Yawn.

Tom, on the other hand, started his software demonstration by taking out a stack of five prescriptions that he had copied when visiting the pharmacy. He would ask,

"Mr. Pharmacist, I'm going to process these prescriptions using our software. Would you please note the time on that clock on the wall?

"We're starting at 10:05."

Tom picked up the first prescription and began,

> The software notifies me that this prescription has an expired insurance plan, so you're going to require cash payment. If I recall, Mr. Pharmacist, you estimate that you are losing $2,500 per month on expired plans.
>
> On this next prescription, I'm going to substitute a brand name when the generic is not in stock, increasing your profit by $3.25 on just one subscription.
>
> Woah. Remember that costly lawsuit you faced last year? That would not have happened. The software just identified a potential drug interaction. You or one of your pharmacists will speak with the doctor before filling the prescription.
>
> This next prescription is a narcotic, so the software notifies you to require a photo identification.
>
> And your fifth prescription is the last refill, so your pharmacist can ask if your customer wants you to request a refill from their doctor. Customers almost always say yes and you lose no continuity to monthly refill cash flow.
>
> Notice the clock. It's 10:10.

Tom waited a moment. A long moment. It gave the pharmacist time to digest what he had seen.

Tom continued, "Okay, we just processed five prescriptions faster than the time it currently takes your pharmacists to process just one. And, by the way, in real life, customers leave when they are frustrated with long lines. The speed of processing prevents that from happening."

Tom summed it up with success stories.

He said, "One pharmacy who bought our software last August increased the average number of prescriptions filled per month by 20%.

Another pharmacy, similar in size to yours, reduced collections from 70 days to 25. The owner of the pharmacy estimates that is worth $60,000 annually."

Tom demonstrated how his software solved pharmacists' pressing business challenges. He focused on the features and benefits that mattered. He spoke the pharmacists' language. And he presented success stories.

By just demonstrating basic features and benefits, I lost the sale even though my software had the same functionality and *was less expensive!*

Demonstrating versus training

Kevin Maxwell is a quota overachiever. He sells software that enables large financial institutions to make sense of their *big data*.

I observed Kevin delivering a software demonstration. Purchasing team member Dina Shoar, Senior Director of Client Services, asked, "Can you show me how to download a dataset from our high-net-worth clients?"

Kevin avoided the training trap. Here is how.

He told Dina, "It's quite simple. During our new customer training, I'll have you actually download several different datasets. What would you like to do with the datasets from your high-net-worth clients?" Notice, he did not show Dina how to download a dataset. That would be training. Kevin's job is to persuade people to buy his software, not teach them how to use it. Here's why he's a top producer:

Dina said, "We'd like to give our high-net-worth clients an extra level of service, but we need to make sure the cost of the extra service doesn't erode our profit margins."

"Why do you want to provide them with an extra level of service, and why now?" Kevin asked with sincere concern. It was clear that he truly wanted to understand Dina's challenge.

Dina thought for a moment. She sighed and rolled her eyes. In a frustrated tone, she said, "We need to out-service a new competitor. We're losing too many clients to them. Last quarter we lost the largest number of clients ever."

"Have you calculated the cost of the lost clients?" Kevin inquired.

Dina did not look happy. "Hundreds of thousands," she whispered.

Kevin responded, "Okay, let's take a look at a dashboard that will solve your problem."

Kevin brought up a dashboard and explained how it had a color-coded, graphical representation of datasets, including high-net-worth clients. He discussed how Dina could slice and dice the dataset to make cost to service level comparisons and ensure profitability. Kevin had a conversation about solving the business challenge. He didn't spend much time on the keyboard. Then he said, "When you attend new customer training, your instructor will teach you how to set up a dashboard that delivers the datasets you want to see, in a format that you want to see them in."

Kevin asked, "What are your thoughts regarding how our software could prevent the loss of high-net-worth clients and hundreds of thousands of dollars to your competition?"

"This would be perfect!" Dina exclaimed.

As usual, Kevin won the sale.

Afterwards, Kevin explained his thinking behind his demonstrations.

"We can enable our clients to make cents of all of their data. That's c-e-n-t-s. Actually, it's typically hundreds of thousands of dollars, not cents!" he said with contagious enthusiasm. "When I demonstrate my software, I want purchasing team members to know how my software solves their pressing business challenges and how they make money because of my software."

Kevin told me that he never *gets stuck in the weeds*. He explained, "Prospects always ask to see features. Before I demonstrate a feature, I need to know why they want to see it. Often, I don't need to show them anything. We just have a conversation about their business challenge and how our software makes it go away."

Like Kevin, when prospects ask, "How does your software do this or that?" be sure you understand the *why* behind their question.

Before demonstrating a particular feature, you are often better off asking, "What would you like to accomplish? Why? How would accomplishing that make life easier or better?

Often, there will be no reason to demonstrate a feature of the software. Your conversation about how life will be better because of your software is all that is needed.

Your experience and intuition come into play here. You should demonstrate a number of features and discuss the associated benefits, so your prospects get a feel for your software. But you do not have to show your prospects how to do everything they ask. That would be training, not persuading to buy!

A good software demonstration makes people feel bad

Sonya Terpeli sells truck-dispatching software. A top producer, Sonya told me, "My best software demonstrations make people feel bad."

"Okay, would you elaborate on that statement?" I asked, curious as to how making someone feel bad helped her sell software.

"It's simple. I want my prospects to dread going back to their desks and having to deal with their business challenges the same old way, now that they know what a difference our software would make," Sonya explained. "Most of my prospects have cumbersome procedures in place to keep their trucks rolling and making money. They typically have multiple systems to maintain driver schedules, perform regular maintenance, invoice customers, comply with the Department of Transportation, and route trucks. When I demonstrate my software, I continually compare how they do things today, without our software, to how they will be able to do things once they own our software. So, when they get back to their desks, all they can think about is how klutzy and inefficient their systems are," Sonya said with a mischievous smile on her face.

Sonya summed it up, "That's what I mean when I say my best demonstrations make people feel bad!"

When demonstrating software, you have to connect the dots between your solution and your prospects' reality – their pressing business challenges. You need to show them how life today is miserable and life tomorrow, with your software, is magnificent.

Discuss life with and without

Bob Leonard sells software to manage nursing homes. He is a top producer. He had a similar philosophy to Sonya. He called it his two-step discussion format.

Bob said, "During my demonstrations, I continually discuss how life is today, without my software, compared to how life will be tomorrow with my software."

This is how he articulated his formula:

1. Today, this is your situation (ouch, pain, frustration, cost).
2. Using our software, your situation will be like this (relief, time saved, more money, better life).

Bob's *ouch-pain-frustration-cost* conversation addressed common nursing home management challenges. He talked about meal service shortages, over or under scheduling nurses, outstanding accounts receivables, hassling with insurance companies, family members in need of consultations, maintaining sanitation, and physician backlogs. Then, he explained how his software addresses those challenges.

Whether you prefer to use Sonya's *make them feel bad* approach or Bob's *two-step discussion format* during demonstrations, continually discuss how life is today without your software solution, and show them how life will be when purchasing team members use your software.

Terminology for conversations

Hamza Abdul is a top producer who sells software to manage construction sites. When he demonstrated his software, he promoted his company's knowledge of the construction business and how that translated into better software.

He would make statements like this, "You can't develop software like this unless you truly understand the construction business. You may want to ask our competitors if they even know the difference between concrete and cement."

When you use the terminology of your prospects' business, you distinguish yourself from competitors. People want to buy from people who understand their business.

Hamza used other industry-related terminology while he gave his demonstrations, like slip sheeting, constructability, change orders, current set, transmittals, and RFIs.

In other examples cited earlier, Ed Heon used terminology from the electrical wholesale distribution business. Tom Modeen used terminology that pharmacists use.

A top producer who sells a marketing platform that improves key word ranking uses terminology such as hyper-traffic, striking distance, and emerging and developmental – all terms common to marketers who understand key word management.

I'd tell you the terminology that Adam Burns, the software sales professional who sold molecular modeling software used, but I can't even spell the words!

Salt your conversation with your prospects' industry terminology as you demonstrate how your software solves their business challenges and you will gain a competitive advantage

Risk mitigation

Eric Blumthal is a top producing software sales professional. A 25-year veteran, Eric has a well-rounded background. He has sold software that connects wireless handheld computers with legacy applications; enterprise software to major healthcare, financial services and telco companies; software for bar code data collection and scanning; and software for distribution and logistics. Currently, he sells knowledge-acceleration software.

Eric told me, "The common thread in all software sales is risk mitigation. Regardless of the software you sell, purchasing team members have an underlying fear, *What if this doesn't work?*

Regardless of which application software Eric sells, he assumes prospects want answers to these questions:

- Do I trust this vendor/salesperson to follow through on his commitments post-sale? If things go south during implementation, do I trust the salesperson to be my advocate post-sale?
- What is my Total Cost of Ownership (TCO)?
- How long before this technology becomes obsolete?
- What does adoption look like? What resources are necessary for successful implementation post-sale *and* what resources/processes need to be in place for ongoing successful operation?
- Even if I trust the vendor and the salesperson, do I trust our internal resources to implement successfully and to maintain success post-sale? How will the vendor help me with this process?
- What are the risks (to me/company/others) if this project fails? What are the benefits if it is successful?
- How do the above risks compare to (a) doing nothing (b) an alternative use of capital?

Eric said, "I believe most fear related to software purchasing has to do with failed projects in the past. Helping prospects visualize what post-implementation success will look like creates a sense of ownership (and potentially vendor preference). So, during pre-demonstration discovery, I ask questions and have conversations about purchasing team members' prior experiences. I learn their concerns about purchasing new software. Then I address those concerns head on during my demonstration."

Eric gave me examples of the types of questions he asks:

- Who will be responsible on your side for successful implementation?
- Who is the ultimate owner of implementation success and post-implementation success?
- How much time can users allocate during training and implementation?

- What simultaneous initiatives may be in play that could affect our implementation schedule?

Be sure to include the risk mitigation conversation in your software demonstrations.

Fear of obsolescence

Gordon E. Moore is the co-founder of Intel and Fairchild Semiconductor. In 1965, he wrote a paper predicting that the number of transistors in a dense integrated circuit would double approximately every two years. This calculation is now known as *Moore's Law.*

To translate, computing power grows incredibly fast. I realize that I just told you something you already know, but it is important to remember Mr. Moore's prediction because your prospects, whether they've heard of Moore's Law or not, will have concerns about technology obsolescence.

Programming languages advance and change. Converting old software applications to leverage new programming languages is rarely easy and sometimes impossible.

In the software industry, competitors who develop software applications from the ground up using new programming languages or tools often usurp large players.

Any person with some business tenure using software applications will be aware of this reality. So, assume your purchasing team members, whether they verbalized the thought or not, will want to know why your software is not at risk of obsolescence. It will not matter how your software solves their pressing business challenges if they are fearful of its obsolescence.

Tell success stories

Robert Burke is a top-flight sales professional who sells software that makes it easy for states, cities, or towns to conduct financial transactions with its citizens and businesses.

When asked about his success, Robert said matter-of-factly, "I just tell lots of success stories."

It sounded too easy to me, so I asked him about a sale he had closed recently with the city of Atlanta, GA.

"Prospects need to know we've been there and done that when it comes to resolving their needs," Robert responded. "I told them a success story about Tampa, FL, a city that had similar needs to the city of Atlanta."

I'll summarize because without hearing the enthusiasm in Robert's voice (it was intense), the story may not sound as interesting as hearing him tell it.

During his software demonstration, Robert explained how the City of Tampa had challenges similar to Atlanta. In addition to running a budget deficit, Tampa was chronically behind in property tax collections. Its motor vehicle bureau always had long lines and customer service by phone was abysmal. The business tax division was behind on collection of tax receipts. Even the utilities division, which was responsible for reading over 140,000 water meters, was behind on collections.

Within one year of implementation, the motor vehicle bureau, the business tax division, and the utilities division were up to date on tax receipts and were literally running a budget surplus of 12%!

Robert wrapped it up, "The city published a request for software proposals to enable the collection of taxes online. After a thorough vetting process, Tampa chose our company because we have a track record enabling other cities to collect taxes online, and we could implement the new software faster than any other options they considered."

Robert summed up why he always tells success stories, "Prospective customers need to hear success stories about my existing customers. Success stories are like the icing on a carrot cake. The cake can be tasty. Add the icing and it becomes delicious!"

What should success stories include?

Similar to written customer testimonials discussed earlier, success stories are a verbal, more accentuated version of customer testimonials.

Like Robert's story, your stories should include the following:

- What was the business challenge?
- How and why did the company make the decision to buy from you?
- What has been the measurable (e.g. dollars, numbers, or percentages) result?

Story telling helps prospects understand your software's value proposition in a more tangible way. And besides, who doesn't love a story?

Map process flows

When selling more expensive and more complex enterprise software, creating a map of your prospects' existing processes and comparing it to your software's cutting-edge processes can be very persuasive. I'd put it in the *picture is worth a thousand words* category.

To find examples of process maps, simply search Google Images for "process map." You can view variations of process maps to find a format that works for your situation.

Kendall Conrad is a top producer who sells enterprise resource planning (ERP) software. His application encompasses CRM, inventory management, agile project management, job costing, scheduling, tracking and efficient quality management.

With the assistance of his sales engineer, during pre-demonstration discovery, he maps prospects' processes. During his software demonstration, he provides a visual representation of the process today, without his software, versus the process using his software.

Kendall said, "The conversations that I have regarding process maps is engaging. It helps my prospects *see* the difference between their life today versus their life when they own my software. I believe these conversations are often the reason I win the sale."

I questioned the time involved in this strategy. "Kendall, doesn't it take an awful lot of selling time to map prospects' processes? Is it really worth it?"

"Granted, using process mapping can eat up a lot of sales minutes," he admitted. "So I'm selective about the prospects and processes where I use this strategy. However, after you've done it several times, you get more efficient and it take less time."

Kendall also said that, to his knowledge, none of his competitors use process mapping in their sales process, so he feels it is truly a competitive distinction for him.

Depending on your software's overall value proposition, process mapping can be an effective demonstration strategy. Consider using process mapping in your sales process.

The value of reports

Maryellen Emden sells software to manage fitness centers. She's always on the leaderboard. She told me about a revelation that enabled her to close more sales.

She met one of her local customers for coffee. Part of her success can be attributed to her after-the-sale follow-up and relationship building. By regularly checking in with her customers, Maryellen generates lots of referral business.

"How is the software working for you?" she asked her customer, Vince Gentili, the manager of three regional gyms.

"I just changed the group fitness schedule to increase attendance in each program," Vince replied.

Vince excitedly explained, "The dashboard report flagged low attendance in some classes. I was able to use the data to change the schedules. Now my group fitness attendance is up across the board."

In the fitness center business, high-group-fitness-class attendance always relates to recurring members. Recurring revenue is its lifeblood.

After listening to Vince, Maryellen had a revelation. She realized that she was demonstrating reports generated by her software all wrong. She was showing prospects what was on the reports. She wasn't showing them how they could use the reports to make intelligent business decisions.

She explained how she delivered her old demonstration and compared it to her new demonstration style:

Old demo:

These are your membership reports. You can view membership growth month over month, quarter over quarter, or any way you'd like to see the data. This report shows how much you spend on different types of marketing.

New demo:

This a graphical analysis of new members by ad source. Using this report, you can see that a shift in allocation of your marketing dollars spent on TV ads, print media, direct mail, email, and customer referral programs will generate approximately 12% more first time visitors.

Maryellen didn't just show prospects reports. She showed them how they could use data from the reports to make intelligent, informed business decisions. Maryellen often told the story about the way Vince was able to improve attendance.

During your software demonstrations, explain which reports purchasing team members can run, what information they can learn, and how information can be used to solve their pressing business challenges.

If the purchasing team member(s) need details, show them how certain data may lead them to run a different report, so they can analyze a situation further.

If you know the types of reports they will want in advance, prepare examples.

Help your prospects envision what life would be like if they had your reporting capability at their fingertips.

Stop popping wheelies

A mentor of mine, Mike Fabiaschi, VP of Sales, coined the *popping wheelies* phrase to describe a certain type of software demonstration.

After a day of offsite sales training, Mike treated the team to a cocktail before dinner. He told a group of us about a recent demonstration he witnessed. "While I loved the Sales Engineer's enthusiasm and knowledge of the software, it was like he was popping wheelies. He kept saying, 'Wait, let me show you this one more feature,'" Mike said.

He laughed, "The prospect was looking at his watch, but trying to be polite and show interest. The SE was so excited to show off his software that he didn't even notice the prospects' obvious need to move on."

"He was like a late night TV commercial," Mike said. "But, wait, there's more! Then he *popped another wheelie*."

Don't pop wheelies. Demonstrate relevant features and benefits and explain why and how life will be better with your software.

Gain agreement throughout

Caution: if you apply this strategy the wrong way, prospects may perceive you as *salesy* and not consultative. Not good.

As you progress through your software demonstration, gain agreement with your prospects that what you have shown them will resolve their business challenges. Ask check-in questions like these:

> *How do you feel this would help?*
>
> *Can you see yourself using our software to help with that challenge?*
>
> *Does this work for you?*
>
> *Have you seen any solution that works this well?*

Sometimes your questions will lead to further clarification; other times they will help the prospect finalize his decision – your software provides the best solution.

The frequency of your questions and how you ask them are important. Ask too often and you may be perceived as pushy. Ask in an insincere manner and you may be perceived as, well, insincere.

Slideshows work

We've all been there. A presenter is showing slide after slide. But his presentation is a yawn. Death by PowerPoint.

When developed and delivered correctly, a slideshow is an important and useful part of your software demonstration agenda.

Using a slideshow (i.e. PowerPoint, Keynote) to position the software demonstration is a best practice. It puts everything in context for prospects and enables you to encapsulate the essence of the demonstration, thus gaining your prospect's full attention and interest.

Here are slide topics to consider using:

- Business challenges

  List three or four of your prospect's most pressing challenges and a summary of the consequences those challenges are having on time, money, personal aggravation, or business growth.

- Industry data

  Cite trends, surveys, research facts and figures, pundit quotes, articles, etc. that support the value of your software.

- Graphic representation

  Use a graphic/visual representation or image. It is said that a picture is worth a thousand words. I'm not really sure how many words a picture is worth, but for most people, visual memory is strong. Therefore, showing a graphic representation of life before and after using your software is a powerful communicator! Consider using one of these examples: a before and after process map, a before and after time-to-complete-task table, or a before and after comparison of profit per transaction.

- Cartoon

    Type *funny sales cartoons* into your search engine. You'll find something you can use in your demonstration to create a humorous moment!

Here are best practices to consider as you develop a slideshow to include in your software demonstration.

- Emulate billboard advertisers

    When people are driving by at 60mph, billboard advertisers need to deliver a message with just a few words that are easy to read and understand. Make your slides like billboards. Use a few words, a relevant image, and a lot of whitespace so your prospects can scan it and get the message.

- Emulate movies

    The next time you watch a movie, notice how quickly scenes or camera angles change. They change frequently to maintain visual interest.

    Like movies, your prospects will be more engaged if you move quickly from slide to slide or use slide builds. Avoid displaying any slide for more than one minute.

- Fourth grade

    Regarding the slideshow used to complement her software demonstrations, one top producer told me, "I pretend I'm developing a slideshow for students in the fourth grade."

    Her words, "I keep my slides simple!"

- Optional slide library

    Keep an optional slide library ready for quick and easy access as you progress through your main slide deck.

    Your optional slide library ensures that you are ready to elaborate on topics that are of special interest to your prospects.

- Acid test

    When you think you are ready to go, give your slide deck an acid test. Go back through your slideshow one more time. As you look at each slide, ask these questions to check for conciseness and cohesion:

    o What's the point of this slide? Is it really needed?

- How does this slide fit into the context of my overall message?
- Does this slide logically follow the prior slide? Does it set up the next slide for a smooth transition?

Follow-up slideshow

Once you've prepared your slideshow for your software demonstration, prepare a second slideshow. Your second slideshow is a standalone show. It can be viewed without your presence. It is self-explanatory. It is designed to be viewed by a purchasing team member with no one else present, or a purchasing team member who may use it to *internally sell* her colleague or boss on your behalf.

Learn from Dr. Seuss or TED Talks

Prepare a Dr. Seuss slideshow. Think *Green Eggs and Ham* and *One Fish, Two Fish*... On the pages of his famous books, you saw big pictures with a few, easy-to-read sentences. Prepare a Dr. Seuss slideshow! Strive to cut words and even syllables from all sentences and create pictorial representations of your key messages.

Or think TED Talk. Check out the slides in the majority of TED Talks. Concise. To the point. Pictures and graphics.

Have a conversation instead of showing a screen

Gerhard Gschwandtner, Founder and CEO at *Selling Power Magazine* and Sales 2.0 Conferences, often defines sales as being a *conversation*. I am in complete agreement. In essence, you have a conversation about a prospect's pressing business challenges and discuss solutions.

I have often observed top producing software sales professionals spend the bulk of their demonstration time holding a conversation about how the software solves business challenges. They knew about their prospects' daily tasks and associated challenges. They talked the prospects' language. They knew what kept them awake at night. And they knew how they got a raise or got fired.

Leveraging this knowledge, top producers had in-depth conversations about how their prospects' life would be better once they owned their software. They persuaded people to buy the software, but only demonstrated select features and functionality of the software.

During your software demonstrations, be sure to spend time *not* showing a screen. Instead, have a conversation about how your software will make a difference.

Superfecta

Some software saves time. For example, manufacturing software can cut a process from 12 hours to 3 hours.

Some software saves money. For example, open-source software (OSS) is free.

Some software increases productivity, hence revenue. For example, call center software prompts up-selling and cross-selling.

Some software improves customer service. For example, self-service software provides assistance on websites.

Software that delivers on all four counts, is equivalent to winning a superfecta at the race track!

During your demonstrations, if possible, be clear about how your software accomplishes all four results.

Sell the implementation process

Tim McClellan, who sells software to manage global life insurance companies, explained:

> To implement our software, a customer has to complete a complex data conversion and validation process, send employees to extensive training, ensure they pass a mandated certification, run dual systems for a quarter, and document the entire process. When we discuss the implementation process during my software demonstration, I can see it in their eyes; they are overwhelmed.

> Prospects can want, need, and afford my software, and then not buy it. Even though their business challenge is pressing, they can always find a reason to wait a month or a quarter.

I asked Tim to elaborate on how he closed so many sales under those circumstances. (He was always on the leaderboard.)

> I face the facts head on and tell them they'll never be ready. My statement always gives them pause. I explain my experience working with so many life insurance companies and why there will never be a perfect time to implement our software. I tell them that while it's a complex and lengthy implementation process, they only do it once and then they'll be using the software to solve their challenges. And then I show them this.

Tim held up a slide with a visual representation of a software implementation process. At a glance, I could see that Tim's implementation team did the majority of the work. His customer's *work* was laid out in steps that were easy to follow and never involved more than three sequential hours.

There were two columns listing responsibilities and timelines: one column for his implementation team, the other for his prospect's team. It was even color-coded.

The visual representation made the implementation process easy to understand, identifying who was responsible for what and completion dates for each step in the process. It looked simple, not complex. Even though the overall timeline was lengthy, it felt *doable*. It also revealed that it was Tim's team who did the heavy lifting.

Tim said, "I reassure my prospects that our implementation team has performed dozens of successful implementations with many different insurers. They appreciate my honesty and they say, sometimes hesitantly, 'Okay, let's do it!'"

Presenting a realistic implementation plan in this manner demonstrates clearly how your software solves your prospects' pressing business challenges.

What you can do today

- Review the prospects in your pipeline and assess your understanding of their challenges. Are they pressing?
- Select three common challenges that your software solves. Review your approach to demonstrating how to solve those challenges. Are you showing prospects how to use the software or are you demonstrating to solve their challenges?
- Select one of the many strategies outlined for demonstrating how your software solves pressing business challenges, and try it.

---

4. Present why your software is better than any other options

Your team is your unfair competitive advantage

It's not ABC Software competing against XYZ Software. It's the *people* at ABC Software competing against the *people* at XYZ Software.

Companies are people. All companies started because a person, or a few people, had an idea. They had a product or service they believed would appeal to people, usually because it solved a problem.

Think about what happens at all companies. People meet. They strategize ideas. They implement the ideas. They regroup. They repeat the process.

Two companies could be founded at the exact same time. Both companies solve the same business challenge. But one becomes an industry leader. Why? The people at that company strategized and implemented better than the people at the second tier company.

Stroll through history. There was the Betamax or VHS videotape format. There was the CP/M or DOS operating system. There was fax or email, and so on!

In the quest for sales, in all cases, the people at one company won and the people at another company lost. You could argue one company had better brand awareness, better funding, better technology, or better user adoption. But the company only had these advantages because the *people* at the company did a better job at strategizing and implementing ideas. After they implemented ideas, they regrouped to discuss what worked and to identify ways to improve further.

As a software sales professional, it is incumbent on you to work proactively with the people at your company to continually develop and refine how you competitively position your software. The people at your company are your competitive advantage.

Your prospect has four options

Dino Scarpinato is a top producer who sells software to manage marinas. He loves his job. In addition to making the money of a quota achiever, Dino gets to spend his days at fancy marinas surrounded by yachts and palm trees.

Dino said he liked to keep things simple. "My prospects only have four options regarding a purchase decision," he explained.

I waited for Dino to sip his club soda and cranberry. I was having an on-the-job conversation with him. We were sitting outside under an umbrella at a waterfront marina restaurant, Dino's new customer.

"Brian," he said, "prospects can do nothing and remain status quo. They can develop a software solution internally. They can purchase from a competitor. Or, they can buy from me."

I asked Dino how he closed this sale with his new customer, who, by-the-way, was footing the bill for our little luncheon.

"During my first conversation, it was apparent that remaining status quo was not an option," Dino said.

He continued, telling me it was clear the prospect had significant management challenges that needed to be resolved, now. That left developing internally or buying from a competitor.

"This marina has a great IT team, but they're stretched, mostly because their existing system is broken! That took doing it themselves off the table," Dino laughed. The marina's only remaining option was to purchase a software solution from Dino or one of his primary competitors.

Dino obviously made the sale. More on how Dino took out his competitors later. Let's discuss the three worst options for you.

The three worst options

Your prospects are always asking themselves, "What is the best option?"

The three worst answers prospects might select are the following:

1. Do nothing and stay with the status quo
2. Develop a software solution internally
3. Purchase from a competitor

An analogy. Whether you are purchasing a desk lamp or an automobile, selecting a new hair stylist or choosing a carpet cleaning service, regardless of whether you are in the market for a product or a service – when you are the buyer, you want to know that you are selecting the best option for your needs.

Whether your prospects verbalize it or not, they want to know, "Is this software the best option for my needs?"

It is incumbent upon you to answer the *best option* question for them! Be clear and specific as to why your software is better than remaining with the status quo, developing internally, or purchasing from competitors.

You only get a commission check for option four: they purchase *your* software!

The do nothing and stay with the status quo option

Picture your purchasing team members sitting at a table with a stack of money. Next to them is a list of options for which they can spend their money. They can hire a new employee, move to a larger office, buy a new phone system, try a different online marketing strategy, attend a tradeshow, or buy your software.

They can take some money off their stack and hand it over to someone else in exchange for something on the list.

Of course, they can do nothing and just keep adding to their stack of money. Maybe they're thinking of saving more for a rainy day or maybe they're thinking of waiting until they have a big enough stack to sponsor a racecar!

The point is, doing nothing regarding the purchase of your software and remaining status quo is often an option that is being considered. If you suspect this is the case, know that during your software demonstration you must help prospects understand that keeping the stack of money on their table is not a smart decision. Show them that if they give you money for your software, they will end up with a significantly larger stack of money and they will have removed the pain they're currently experiencing.

Note: If you're selling software where the status quo is not an option (e.g. legal compliance requirements, expiring software licenses, user capacity issues, or a myriad of other catalysts for interest), consider yourself fortunate! One bad option is off your prospects' checklists.

The develop a software solution internally option

Generally speaking, software developers think they're smart. And they deserve to think that way. Have you ever tried writing code that actually *does* something? But sometimes they think they are so smart, they can simply develop software themselves that will accomplish what your software accomplishes. *Sometimes*, they really can.

Therefore, you need to persuade prospects that purchasing your software is better than developing it in-house.

Often referred to as the *build versus buy* decision, you need to make a case for the value of services that come with your software. Here are some examples of features and benefits of services that will mitigate the option of developing in-house:

- Ongoing new releases, which offer even better feature functionality
- New hire and ongoing training to ensure everyone leverages all the value your software offers
- Process documentation so that all employees understand how to use the software
- Support delivered rapidly by experienced professionals, minimizing business interruptions
- Access to knowledge of best practices because your company's sales, marketing, and product development teams are focused full time on understanding the industry and its trends
- Continual leveraging of new programming technology to improve business results
- Access to user groups and participation in feature development prioritization

In addition to making a case for the value of services, sometimes the most compelling argument against developing in-house is the following: if an IT team works on developing software, what will they *not* be doing? IT professionals are expensive and in short supply. IT teams are notoriously understaffed, lacking enough developers to get everything done that needs to be done. So be sure to have the *what's-not-getting-done* conversation with your prospect as well.

Mark your calendar

If you lose an opportunity to the develop-in-house proposal, mark your calendar for a follow up. Often, after a prospect attempts the develop-internally approach, it fails. Once your prospect has a failure scar, he is ready to discuss purchasing software again.

The purchase from a competitor option

In the early days of voice recognition software, I observed a top producer take out her competition. It was fun!

Gina Phelps sold voice recognition software. During a demonstration to a warehouse management team, Gina showed how her software maximized truck loading time and saved hundreds of thousands of dollars annually.

At that time, the software only recognized key words that were pre-programmed. The forklift operator would speak into a microphone as he was loading a truck, "Pallet ten loaded. Break time." The software would recognize "ten" and "break time."

Gina discussed how the forklift operator verbally submitted pertinent data that was automatically delivered to the warehouse management, inventory management, and transportation management team members. Armed with the data, management was able to increase profits, reduce inefficiencies, and gain a competitive advantage.

At the time, there were only three vendors that offered such a solution.

Gina asked the audience of five purchasing team members, "Would you like to hear about some of the unique functionality we offer compared to our competitors?"

Of course, they answered *yes*.

She then listed the names of her two competitors and her company's name on the whiteboard. Underneath, she listed features in each column, stating, "All software will offer this, this, and this feature. However, our software also enables you to..."

Not an exact replica, but the whiteboard looked like this:

Competitor A	Competitor B	Gina's Company
voice recognition	voice recognition	voice recognition
auto transcription	auto transcription	auto transcription
data recall	data recall	data recall
6000' range	6000' range	6000' range
	remote location support	remote location support
		multi lingual – all employees can use it
		database integration – prevents corrupt data
		multi user included – lower cost
		user group driven – continual improvement

Without reading, just by looking, it's easy to recognize that Gina's software offers greater functionality than her competitors'.

Of note, when Gina listed her software's four additional features, she also listed the *benefits*. She explained, "I always talk about the benefits of our additional features. In the 'we all have it' category, I only mention features."

To be a top producer, you need to be able to drive home your software's unique value proposition compared to your competitors'.

It was a terrific visual representation of her software's unique benefits.

She won the sale. She made her competitor's life difficult!

Competition is compounded

When selling Software as a Service (SaaS), if the solutions are nice to have, but not essential, your competition is compounded.

Let's say you sell a SaaS solution to manage and track sales proposals. Your prospects, typically VPs of Marketing and VPs of Sales, have the standard three buckets of competition: do nothing and remain status quo, develop a software solution internally, or purchase from a competitor.

But they also have other SaaS solution vendors knocking on their door, all claiming to save time, increase revenue, or improve customer service within the marketing and sales function. Your prospects are receiving sales calls regarding appointment scheduling software, knowledgebase software, sales enablement solutions, predictive dialer solutions, expense management software, and so on. So your competition is compounded by all these other nice to have solutions.

Focus your sales proposal on your software's strengths – compared to all other solutions (not just your proposal management software competitors), your software makes good business sense.

Note: at the time of this writing, on average, solutions of this nature cost $40 per month per user. I had a Regional VP of Sales tell me, "If one more salesperson says, 'It's just $40 per month. That's less than a cup of coffee per salesperson per day,' I'll shoot them."

He explained that every salesperson had a story about how low the cost was. "I'm up to 9 SaaS licenses for 80 salespeople in my region. That's almost $30 grand a month!"

So use the *only $40 per month* argument carefully.

The busy restaurant theory

Imagine you and your date decide to try a new restaurant. You check some online reviews and select a restaurant. You drive to the restaurant at 7:30 Friday evening. When you pull into the parking lot, you see only six cars.

What are you likely thinking? *Hmm, nobody's here. I wonder if this place is any good?*

Let's replay the scenario. You drive to the restaurant at 7:30 Friday evening. When you pull into the parking lot, it's packed.

What are you likely thinking? *Wow, this place must be great!*

When a restaurant is busy, customers assume it must be good. The busy restaurant theory applies to software sales as well.

When you are selling software, you want to create that same *in demand* image. Prospects prefer to buy from companies that appear to have many other customers. *Everyone's doing it. It must be good.*

Whether or not you have a line of prospective customers out your door ready to buy, you can create the impression that you do. Never lie, but appear busy. Here are five examples of how to leverage the busy restaurant theory:

1. When scheduling appointments, offer a few select time slots instead of saying your calendar is open. If a prospect asks you to meet at 2:00pm, ask if 2:15 is okay.
2. Use an online calendar tool to show your available timeslots. Be sure to have a number of timeslots blocked off.
3. Consider the phraseology you use. Sound like you are a high growth, busy company because everyone is buying your software. Try one of these examples:

   > *I can't tell you how many VPs I've spoken with in the last quarter who have the same challenge.*

   > *Six of my newest customers told me…*

   > *I meet new employees here every day.*

   > *Attendance at our annual customer conference has been growing 25% a year.*

4. When discussing your new customer on-boarding schedule, speak as if securing a date early is important.
5. Don't answer your phone immediately and, sometimes, don't even answer. Of course, you need to respond in a timely manner, but think of the perception you are giving compared to a competitor who answers on the first ring every time a prospect calls.

Perception matters in software sales. Always give the impression that every smart executive wants to purchase your software.

Timing the demonstration, let your competitors go first

To use an analogy, FIFO and LIFO are accounting methods used to value the cost of goods sold. FIFO is an acronym for the term, "first in, first out." LIFO is an acronym for the term, "last in, first out." You can account for inventory one way or the other, but not both.

Ideally, when demonstrating software, you want to be in a FILO position: first in, last out.

Be the first to discuss your software with your prospect and provide an executive summary of your value proposition, but wait to be the last to provide a software demonstration.

When you are first in, you have an opportunity to set the stage, discuss evaluation criteria, and predispose the prospect to your solution. Provide prospects with information to get them thinking about selection criteria when evaluating options. Get them excited about your upcoming software demonstration, but try to schedule it after your competitors schedule their demonstrations.

Being last to demonstrate will work to your advantage because prospects tend to better remember the software they have seen most recently. Your demonstration will be top-of-mind when purchasing team members meet to discuss their plans. Additionally, once purchasing team members have seen competitors' software, they will be more knowledgeable about software solutions, ask more well-informed questions, and develop clarity about the importance of your software features and benefits.

Using FILO, also supports the busy restaurant theory. "Mr. Prospect, we've had so much interest in our software that the next available demonstration timeslot is in two weeks."

Sell the quality of post implementation support

Harrison Wilson sells software in a highly competitive environment. He sells Customer Relationship Management Software (CRM).

Although historically he had been a top producer, he floundered for a year before reaching his stride at his new job. Then, he was back on the leaderboard.

Harrison said:

> Between the popularity of one major-league competitor and at least fifty decent other competitors, it's hard to distinguish CRM software. It's easy to get in a price war. While some have better user interfaces, others have better social media tie ins; others have better data capture; others integrate with marketing platforms; and so on. Prospects can easily perceive that we all do the same basic thing: enable salespeople to track contacts and opportunities.

However, Harrison's company had a unique approach to customer service. It provided up to three hours of secretarial support per month. Rather than tell prospects about it, however, Harrison had them experience it.

During his demonstrations, he would put up a slide with five scenarios:

1. Sales rep in the field driving between appointments. No time to enter data into CRM.
2. VP Sales stuck in airport. Too tired to log on to see important sales stats.
3. CEO in Board meeting. Needs details on sales transactions.
4. VP Marketing in partner meeting. Needs stats on new prospect sources.
5. Sales operations rep on tradeshow floor. Needs product descriptions.

He asked the purchasing team members to pick a scenario. He then dialed his customer support line on the speakerphone and performed a mock service call.

In the scenario where the sales rep needed data entered, the support team member typed the data into the CRM while the rep spoke.

In the scenario where the VP Sales needed important stats, the *secretary* read them off.

In the scenario where the CEO was in the Board meeting, the *secretary* provided the details on sales transactions.

In the scenario where the VP Marketing needed stats, the *secretary* looked them up.

In the scenario where a sales ops rep was on the tradeshow floor, the *secretary* read the product descriptions.

Harrison always gave the support team a heads-up so they were prepared for the secretarial support call.

Harrison persuaded customers that all CRM software had to enable salespeople to track contacts and opportunities. What distinguished his company was how its support team enabled customers to make the most use of their investment.

Interestingly, customers rarely used the secretarial support, but when they did, it provided useful insights for the product development team regarding ways to make the software even more valued in the real world.

If you make a case for your post implementation support, whether secretarial service or some other advantage, you distinguish your software from competitors.

Note: If your company thinks secretarial support would provide a competitive advantage, it's easy to pilot with select prospects. Track the usage and cost and validate that secretarial support can be cost effective.

Competitive intelligence

In order to demonstrate why your software is better than the competitors' software, monitor them often and closely. Here are some easy ways to do that.

Ask new customers

> Ask your customers what caused them to select your software. They will tell you. During those conversations, delve deeply. Ask if there were particular features or functionalities that they liked about your competitors' software. Ask if they will share their selection criteria. Ask which competitors they eliminated early on and why. Ask if competitors had sales approaches they particularly liked. Ask, ask, and ask. It can't hurt to ask. The worst that can happen is they will not want to tell you. It's not as if you'll lose them as a customer. You'll be surprised how much you can learn.

> One top producer told me she always asks a simple open-ended question, "What can you tell me about our competition that may help me be a more effective salesperson?"

She said she's received copies of competitors' proposals, evaluation checklists, price comparison charts, feature lists, salesperson contact information, results of reference checks, and more.

Monitor websites

Review competitors' websites, *regularly*. Ideally, your Marketing team will have an automated approach to monitoring competitors' websites. You need to know about new product releases, online marketing demos, tradeshow schedules, investor relations, and the like *as they happen*. You need to be prepared to respond to prospects' questions about your competitors' latest shenanigans!

Get on email list

Sign up for your competitors' newsletters and marketing emails.

Of note, I don't sign up for my competitors' email marketing in stealth mode using a personal email. I don't believe it is necessary. Some people prefer using an alias.

Search engine alerts

Set alerts in your search engines for competitors' names or names of competitors' employees.

LinkedIn and Twitter

Search LinkedIn for competitors' company LinkedIn page.

Follow competitors' executives on Twitter.

How much time you invest acquiring competitive intelligence compared to how much time you spend learning your prospects' business challenges is part of the art-of-the-sale. Done right, it will not take much time for you to stay current about the ways your competitors position their offerings. Armed with this knowledge, you can do a much better job distinguishing your company and your software from your competition.

Competitive positioning

Our Moms said, "If you have nothing nice to say about someone, don't say anything."

It is hard to disagree with Mom's logic and it applies during your software demonstration. Disparaging statements about competitors are unprofessional. They cause prospects to question your credibility and be suspect of your integrity.

That said, it is appropriate to discuss areas where you believe your solution out performs or compares favorably with your competition. In fact, as discussed earlier, prospects *want* to know why your software is the best option. That's why they're at the demo!

Communicate your strengths compared to other options in a non-disparaging, professional manner.

Here are generic variations of phrases that enable you to communicate why your software is the best option, without being disparaging:

Our customers tell us they selected us over ABC Company because…

We recently incorporated this feature because we listened to what business people like you told us. To our knowledge, we are the only software solution available that can do this for you...

When we survey our customers to find out what caused them to select our software, we consistently hear our xyz feature is the best. This enables our customers to… [benefit].

Based on our recent research, no other software on the market is capable of [unique feature] so that you will be able to [benefit].

I've worked in this industry over X years. I've never seen a competitor who can [unique function] and [unique function] and [unique function].

A primary difference between our competitors and us is that our approach to [solving problem] involves [unique solution].

One reason [new customer similar to prospect] selected us after using ABC Company's software was that we solved this [business problem].

We've received accolades by [noteworthy source] for being the best…

In each statements, the seller is able to distinguish his unique value proposition in a manner that is professional and believable without saying anything directly negative about a competitor.

Lauren Kelley sells software to manage biotech research. A top producer, Lauren told me, "My purchasing team members consist of mostly scientists and engineers. Not only do they want to know how our software compares to my competition, they need reassurance that our company is the foremost, preeminent, undisputed leader!"

Here is a list of competitive positioning statements that Lauren crafted:

We've been working in the biotech industry for over a decade.

We have over 50 biotech firms using our software in Europe alone.

Over 85% of our customers converted from competitive systems.

Since we started 10 years ago, we've lost track of all the competitors that have come and gone.

Seven of the top ten largest biotech firms use our software. The other three have homegrown systems.

When scientists who use our software move to another research firm, they often advocate for our software.

Scientists have told us that the biggest mistake they've made was not buying our software years ago.

Research labs accelerate drug-to-market time by an average of 20% using our software.

When using our software, you have virtually no more administrative tasks.

Scientists have told us that our software makes them so efficient; it is equivalent to adding another scientist to their team.

Our research and development department is regularly awarded grants from the US government.

Use these examples to create your own competitive positioning statements.

Play it safe and role-play your competitive positioning statements with a peer. Your peer can tell you whether you may be crossing the line and saying something that isn't nice. Make Mom proud!

Rapid and relevant follow-up

Picture your prospect returning to his desk the morning after your demonstration. While perusing his email over morning coffee, he reads the following email from you.

Subject: Answers to your questions and additional information

Bill,

Regarding your question about the security of our data center, our Chief Security Officer, Jim Bridge, said the data center does have a level one clearance.

Also, check out this article in last month's *Security Center Magazine*. Susan Price, author of the new book, *How Secure is Your Company's Data?* gives an interview. She talks about the importance of level one clearance.

I look forward to next Wednesday's conference call with your team. I'm confident they will like the implementation plan you and I discussed.

Regards,

John

They also read an email from a competitor. They had seen his demonstration a week prior.

Subject: Touching base

Bill,

It was good to meet you last week.

I wanted to touch base and see if you need any more information.

Take care,

Lewis

Your email was rapid and relevant. Your competitor's email was, well, need I comment?

If you want to distinguish yourself from the competition, follow up immediately after your demonstration with information that is of value to your prospect.

In addition to email, consider using traditional mail. Picture prospects opening a package or a letter from you. Before they even know what you sent, you've conjured an image of professionalism. And your competitor has not.

Rapid and relevant follow-up adds one more notch to your prospects' competitive measurement stick!

You may have a strong competitor who also does a great job demonstrating her software. Upon conclusion of both demonstrations, your prospect may be thinking, *Wow, two good companies.* But your professional follow-up can change the game and make your prospect feel better about purchasing your software.

Take primary competitors on immediately

Jane Hertford sells software to manage restaurants. DineSoft, the gorilla in her industry, had name recognition and market share.

A top producer, Jane knew that her prospects would be viewing a DineSoft demonstration.

I asked Jane how she competes.

She said, "At the beginning of my software demonstration, I say, 'Here is what distinguishes our software from DineSoft.' I need to take on DineSoft immediately. Most of my prospects are already inclined to choose it because it is the industry leader. They need to know why we are better."

Sometimes referred to as *column fodder*, prospects may view a demonstration of your software to make sure they can say they looked at all of the options. However, they may already be planning to buy from the industry leader.

Jane tells her prospects, "While DineSoft is well-known software, our software addresses certain restaurant management challenges much better." She tells them that her software, unlike DineSoft, is designed from the ground up to increase table turns, a common key performance indicator for restaurants. The more tables you serve in a night; the more money you make. For purchasing team members, whose restaurants consider table turns a key performance indicator, Jane gets their attention.

Jane also talks about why her company was founded. "When we began, there was no software that was built from the ground up, which increased table turns. The two founders owned five restaurants. They knew that the more meals they served in a night, the more money they would make. But they could not find software that addressed the table turn challenges." She mentions existing customers who used to use DineSoft and why they switched to her software. She cites examples of customers whose table turns increased within two months of going live.

Jane says, "I take my primary competitor head on. I answer the question that I know all my prospects have, whether they verbalize it or not, 'Why is your software better than DineSoft?'"

Jane observes prospects' reactions during her competitive positioning conversation. She says that she can *get a read* as to whether they will give her software serious consideration. If there is only mild interest in improving table turns and it appears they have made up their minds and are favoring DineSoft, she accelerates through her demonstration. She explains that she'd rather spend her time with prospects who have a higher likelihood of buying.

When prospects have a predisposition for an established competitor, take the competitor on immediately. If you can't gain agreement on your competitive advantages, you can't win the sale. Cut your losses early.

Use endorsements

If a key association endorses your product, if an industry expert gives it accolades, if you have reference letters, if someone in your firm has been published, or if a positive article about your software has been written – these are all endorsements. Reference them during your demonstrations.

If you do not have endorsements, get them as soon as you can.

Prospects need to hear that objective industry experts think your company and your software is great.

Referencing endorsements during your software demonstration adds credibility to your value proposition. It is a competitive advantage.

LinkedIn profiles count

Savvy prospects do their research. Assume they will view LinkedIn profiles of people who work at the companies they are considering doing business with. Well-written LinkedIn profiles can help you gain a competitive advantage. Make sure yours is more impressive than your competitors'.

Have your marketing team give employees guidance for writing effective LinkedIn profiles, or even offer to assist them by writing drafts or editing.

Setting traps for the competition

Renat Adilov sells a marketing platform application. He is a top producer.

When I met Renat a few years back, he told me, "Marketing platforms are relatively new, so I position our company as a leader in research regarding the future of marketing platforms."

Marketing platforms take many shapes and sizes. In general, a marketing platform engages a prospective customer online and leads him through his buying process. It leverages content (e.g. inbound marketing) or paid advertising to attract potential customers and drive website traffic through an educational and self-qualifying process. Ultimately, marketing platforms drive targeted prospects to websites and, over time, convert them to qualified prospects so the sales team can win their business.

After explaining his company's comprehensive approach to developing new features and functionality based on customers' needs and market demand, he tells prospects, "Ask our competitors about their approach to developing new features. I'm confident you'll find ours is the best."

Renat's company's approach to ongoing development of its software features deploys comprehensive and measurable voice-of-the-customer studies, pilots new features with select marketers, and runs A/B testing. Potential customers view his company as risk free. They feel assured that his software will always be the "latest, greatest" and that they'll never be disappointed because they've purchased software that was behind the times.

Renat told me, "I try to set the standard for how purchasing team members evaluate our software." He laughed, "It's kind of like setting traps for my competitors. I know they don't have a comprehensive sales presentation regarding product development."

Remember the old adage, "The best defense is a good offence."

To set traps for competitors, make the case for your strengths and persuade your prospects to investigate how competitors address the same issue.

This is the art-of-the-sale. Never bad-mouth your competition. That is simply not professional. However, you can persuade your prospects to keep certain selection criteria on their short list.

Maintain a winning mindset

We've all heard stories of sports professionals using visualization techniques to improve their performance during the game. Athletes will imagine a scene, complete with images of a previous best performance or a future desired outcome. They are instructed to simply *step into* that visualization and feel the emotions they are experiencing. While imagining these scenarios, the athlete imagines the details and the way it feels to perform in the desired way.

Legendary golfers Jack Nicklaus and Tiger Woods practiced each shot in their mind before taking it. Russian Olympic athletes, who were coached to mentally rehearse their performance, performed better than those who did not. One study showed that people who carried out virtual weight training workouts increased their muscle strength compared to those who did not. Visualization improves performance.

You can use visualization to improve your software demonstration performance as well.

Rehearse your demonstration in your mind. Picture your prospects actively engaged in conversation about their business challenges. Hear yourself professionally take out the competition. Imagine prospects saying, "Let's do it!" at the conclusion of your demonstration. Maintain a winning mindset. Intend to win the sale.

Use visualization prior to your software demonstration. Envision your prospects responding enthusiastically to your presentation and your discussion about your software's superiority.

You've been there and done that

Prospects need to know you've *been there and done that* in terms of working with companies or people in positions similar to them. Salt your conversation with phrases that help clients feel you understand their industry and their role.

Here are some examples:

> *We hear that all the time from the xyz companies we work with.*
>
> *One of the things we hear most from our customers in your industry is…*
>
> *CMOs that we've worked with like that our software enables them to…*
>
> *All I do every day is speak with people in your industry, and a common theme is…*
>
> *Just last month, I was working with Bill Smith, who's a director of ABC. He had the exact same challenge. What we found was…*
>
> *The finance teams are always excited about…*

You gain a competitive advantage when prospects feel that you understand their situation because you have extensive experience working with people and companies that are similar.

This is particularly important when competitors' software has similar features and functionality in their software. If prospects perceive that your software's capability and general price range are equal to the competitors', the fact that you and your company have a broader and deeper understanding of their industry and job function will tip the scale heavily in your favor.

Competitive positioning by purchasing team profiles

If you are selling to a purchasing team, it's important to consider your software's competitive advantages in relation to the purchasing team members' profile.

A CFO may be enamored with the feature/functionality of a competitor's software, while a VP of Operations may be enamored with the feature/functionality of a different competitor's software. And for valid reasons!

As you progress through your software demonstration, speak directly to competitive advantages as they apply to purchasing team members' profiles.

Here are some examples:

> *Mary, you'll be particularly interested in this because Chief Technology Officers we work with all struggle with the same challenge of...*

> *Bill, the reason our software lets you do this is because the Directors of Sales we work with tell us they can increase forecast accuracy...*

> *Of all the Purchasing Managers we've surveyed during the last five years, the most common frustrations they express are... Which is why we have this feature...*

In each example, the sales pro spoke to the purchasing team member profile.

Perform a win/loss analysis

Performing a win/loss analysis can provide invaluable competitive information.

A win/loss analysis is the process of talking to prospects who bought and those who did not buy. A win/loss analysis is not simply a survey. While it takes the form of a survey, (either verbal or written, in-person or by phone) it involves analyzing the data to make informed decisions about your marketing, sales, customer service, and product development initiatives.

Done correctly, a win/loss analysis is administered over time. Measurable and sometimes observable goals are established and tracked.

Ideally, outsource your win/loss analysis to a consulting firm. When a professional consulting firm reaches out to prospects who bought and those who did not buy, they respond differently than when you reach out directly. They tend to open up and tell the real story – minute details they are not comfortable sharing with you directly.

As a consultant who performs win/loss analysis, I once learned a competitor used one of his customers as a reference. When contacted, the reference would explain why he stopped using my client's software and had bought from the competitor.

It turns out, this customer-turned-competitor reference was the one and only customer who ever *defected*. He had been known as the customer from hell. A cease and desist letter from my client's attorney put an instant stop to the competitor using this negative reference.

Align sales, service, product development, and marketing

The faster the folks in your product development, marketing, and customer service hear about competitors' advances, the better.

No one in your company is as close to the market as your sales professionals. Salespeople learn the most current competitive information because they are speaking with *prospective*, not existing customers, day in and day out. Salespeople hear about marketplace developments, competitors' strategies, and prospects' business challenges sooner than anyone else at your company.

Develop a process for salespeople to provide rapid marketplace feedback to your product development, marketing, and customer service teams. Those teams can help craft your competitive advantage when they hear what the sales team is learning. One approach is to set up a series of checkbox questions in your CRM. During the opportunity won or lost stage, require salespeople to check a few answers to provide quick and easy feedback.

When your product development, marketing, and customer service teams learn the competitive lay of the land, they are better positioned to develop both your defensive and offensive competitive strategy. For example, being first to market features and functionality that reduce costs, increase revenue, or both, is an offensive strategy. Rapidly responding to a competitive threat is a defensive strategy.

You will be better at defense and offense if you have aligned your product development, marketing, and customer service teams. As a software sales pro, interdepartmental alignment is not your primary responsibility, but participate in it to the best of your ability! Your company's rapid response to competitive threats will enable you to achieve your sales goals.

What you can do today

1. Develop a software demonstration that takes on your competitors.
2. Try it.
3. Regroup and assess what worked and how you can make your demo even more distinguished from competitors.

---

5. Discuss how your software is cost justified

Dollars, Numbers, Percentages

As you demonstrate your software, build dollars, numbers, and percentages into your conversations. Tell prospects how your customers used the software's features to increase revenue from $X to $Y, to shorten time-to-new-hire-productivity from three months to two months, to increase average order size 5%, or whatever metric is relevant.

Your discussion of dollars, numbers, and percentages as you demonstrate your software forms the foundation for building a business case.

Present a conservative ROI

Jennifer Wilson sells software to manage fitness clubs. She is a top producer.

Jennifer told me about a software cost justification presentation that backfired… in a good way. After weeks of corralling members of the purchasing team, she finally met them on a Friday morning, a traditionally slow time for fitness clubs.

She told me the following:

> I got to the business case part of my demonstration. I had a solid ROI presentation. Using their data, I was able to demonstrate a conservative ROI that justified buying my software.
>
> I showed them how they could increase membership by 15% in a year, retain members five months longer, improve outstanding accounts receivable, and avoid hiring another finance team member.
>
> Scott Ashodian, the General Manager, who was the ultimate decision maker, said, 'Jennifer, I disagree with your numbers.'

Jennifer said that her heart sank. She was in disbelief. She had spent hours collecting what she thought was accurate data from them. She had crafted a conservative ROI to make sure the purchasing team members would agree!

Scott said, "I think we could increase membership 20% the first year. I also think retention will be longer."

"Scott argued that my software would enable them to make more money!" Jennifer said delightedly.

Needless to say, Jennifer won the sale.

Present a conservative ROI. Prospects can't argue with your data when you are conservative. Or, if they do argue, it'll be in your favor!

Sometimes you don't need ROI

If you are selling software that is a *must-have*, meaning companies can't operate without it, developing an ROI may not be necessary. In these situations, you need to help prospects get budget approval.

For example, companies *need* accounting software, phone management software, virus protection software, payroll software, and CRM software. You can't run a business without these software applications. In these situations, prospects will need to get budget approval, reallocate funds, or add to next year's budget.

When selling *must-have* software, learn as much as you can about your prospect's budgeting process. Ask questions like these:

> *How do you justify purchasing software?*

How do you get approval for an unbudgeted expense?

What information will be needed to receive an approval?

Who is involved in the budget approval process?

What is your budget approval process?

When does budgeting take place?

What's the cost of not buying the software?

What if the software you want costs more than the competitor's software?

I have assisted many customers in developing their ROI analyses. Can I be involved in developing yours?

Armed with answers to these questions, you can help your primary contact acquire budget and purchase approval.

Emotional ROI

During a recent checkup, my doctor asked me what I do for a living. When I told him I'm a consultant and I help companies sell more software, he launched into a rant about how his practice management software was so hard to use.

I asked if the members of his practice were looking into purchasing new software. He said, "It took us three years to get to where we can use this software. I wouldn't want to do that again! This software is the devil we know. It's working well enough for now. We have too many other things going on to consider going through another implementation headache."

In addition to a business ROI, prospects need an emotional return-on-investment.

In some cases, like my doctor's office, an emotional ROI trumps a business ROI.

Emotional ROI is about fear of risk or change. Buying application software is risky for your prospects. They put their sense of peace and stability at risk when they purchase software. They are concerned about what can go wrong. They question themselves. They have internal conversations. *Maybe the status quo isn't so bad. A lot can go wrong. What if this software doesn't work? How will this affect my job status?*

Your prospects need assurance that your software will work. And, if for any reason it doesn't work, support will be provided to fix the problem immediately. They need to feel the worst that can happen is not so bad at all.

Tell prospects why your solution is the safest.

Purchasing team members are weighing their emotional ROI during your software demonstration. You need to assure them that the emotional benefits they will receive from your software will outweigh the emotional risks present at the time of purchase.

To do this, you need to work with purchasing team members individually. Revisit the information you garnered during your discovery regarding individuals' day-in-the-life-of. Reassure them they will be safe. Should anything go wrong, your support team is unparalleled. They personally will not have to worry. The software will work. Their life will be good!

Purchasing team members will believe in your emotional ROI if they are confident that your software will make their reputation grow, will make them more upwardly mobile, will not put current projects at risk, and will not hurt their outside relationships and interests.

Prospects put their sense of peace and stability at risk when they purchase software. Unfortunately, most tenured business executives can tell you stories about software that didn't do what they needed it to do. So, even though they are familiar with the inefficiencies of their existing situation, they're used to it, and they feel safe.

Tell prospects why your solution is the safest.

Beware of soft ROIs

I had a client who owned a startup software company. Her software was designed to improve efficiency; therefore, it saved time. Its target prospects were single location companies with more than 1000 employees. Using the software, tasks that took many employees two hours now just took two clicks.

Her business case was built on the premise that if all employees had two more hours of time, they would accomplish more work.

The business case didn't work. Prospects didn't buy the premise.

While the logic of her argument makes sense, the reality is different. You can plug some numbers into a spreadsheet and logically discuss productivity per employee hour worked, but finance dudes won't buy it.

Giving an employee an extra two hours to do work each day never correlates directly to lower costs or increased revenue. If you had 1.5 hours more time to sell each day, would you sell 20% more? Doubtful.

When you are having an ROI conversation, certainly refer to improved efficiency and saving time, but put it in the category of a *soft* ROI.

In my client's case, we were able to revise the soft ROI to one that finance dudes bought. We showed how the software deleted expense items from their budget. Using the software meant they did not have to hire as many employees as they had budgeted for.

ROI partnership

Louise Fedder is a quota achiever who sells software to manage the process of bidding on large roadway construction projects. Her software is the most expensive solution.

It's the most expensive for a reason. Every prospect who sees it, wants it. The software is feature rich and her company has a great reputation. The software does everything prospects want bidding software to do, and more.

Inevitably, her prospects need a cost justification. To develop a cost justification, Louise engages with her prospects.

Louise said, "My prospects build roads every day. They don't buy construction management software often, if ever. They appreciate my offer to assist with developing a business case for purchasing our software. I develop a partnership with them. I work with them on their cost/benefit analysis."

She related this example:

> Construction cost estimators on large roadway projects are the lifeblood of the industry. If they nail it, their company wins the bid and makes a significant profit. So, I have conversations about how our software can drive the cost of roadway construction projects down.
>
> I demonstrate how they can compare safety rails designed to rust to more expensive aluminum rails. I demonstrate how they can compare the costs of entrance ramps with traffic lights to entrance ramps with no lights and longer roadways. I demonstrate how they can compare the costs of over-the-road signs to side-road signs.

She gives her prospects a spreadsheet to complete post demo. They enter data from a recent construction bid that they lost. Louise runs the data through her software. During a conference call, she presents her findings, which always show how they could have lowered their bid and maintained their profit margin, or sometimes increase profit!

Louise said, "By the end of the conference call, the fact that my software is the most expensive is no longer an issue."

Develop a partnership with your prospects and assist them with the creation of a business case to purchase your software. They'll appreciate it.

Talk to existing customers about their ROI

Some of the best ROIs come from your existing customers. Talk to your customers one, two, or three years after using your software. Ask them about how they justify the cost. Ask them how they determine whether to keep the software subscription or license fee in their budgets. Use this information to help your prospects craft an ROI.

Trials

If your software lends itself to *trials*, try them! Trials can go a long way towards building a cost justification for the purchase of your software.

Often application software has the *take the puppy home for the weekend, if you don't like him, bring him back* effect. No one brings puppies back.

If this is the case with your software, the conclusion of your demonstration should be an agreement to do a trial. It's an easy next step for your prospect.

Trials, also referred to as pilots, test drives, sandbox (e.g. play in the sandbox), or other names, are all the same. You let prospects try your software with the assumption that they'll like it and buy it.

Trials require resources. If you cannot dedicate resources to support trials, do not do them. They rarely work without support.

I worked with one software company who tried a marketing campaign based on the message, "Take us for a test drive." They soon became the world's leading distributor of test drives. But the test-drive-to-close ratio was abysmal. They did not have the resources to support the test drive process.

To support a trial of your software, do the following:

Position it as a buy and try, not a try and buy

If prospects want to try your software, let them, but under this condition: they *are* buying it, subject to the results of the trial. They are not trying, then buying. They have bought, but they are validating their purchase.

Establish measurable or observable objectives

To *try* your software, prospects must agree on how they will evaluate it. How will they measure or observe success? What will have happened in order for them to agree to purchase? No gray areas allowed.

Agree on a timeline

What are the start and end dates of the trial? Before starting the trial, schedule a review meeting with the appropriate purchasing team members on the end date. You want a date in their calendar. Agree in advance, we'll decide *yes* or *no* on this date.

Trial extension requests

Prospects have a tendency to request trial extensions. When a trial is well-managed, you limit these requests. If you grant an extension to the trial timeline, it should be for unexpected circumstances, such as a purchasing team member needs to be out for a family emergency, not because *we're not sure yet*.

Have trial owners

Agree on who will be the lead person during the trial period on your prospects' side and on your side. Have designees agree on a communication plan. Trial owners need to communicate who'll do what, by when. Then, make sure schedules are adhered to, changes are communicated, and objectives are being tracked.

Pros and cons of trials

Pros

- Over time, you learn, refine, and continue to improve your trial-to-close ratio.
- Managed correctly, when trials fail, often it's for a valid reason and your software would not have been a good fit. So trials enable you to sell to ideal customers.
- Prospects who agree to a trial are serious.

Cons:

- Sales cycles are longer.
- Resources are diverted to support trials.
- Cost of sales increases.

Negotiation strategies

Ideally, the close of a sale is the natural outcome of a well-executed software demonstration process. Upon conclusion of the process, the prospects' logical next step is to purchase your software.

Unfortunately, in real life, it doesn't always work that way.

As persuasive as your conversations may be about your business proposal, ROI, and cost justification, prospects will negotiate. They are trained to ask, "Is that the best you can do?" It's Negotiating 101. They also know that to internally sell this purchase, they will need evidence that they got the best price. Here are some strategies for negotiation in your software sales process. Definitely in the art-of-the-sale category, using these strategies successfully requires timing and tact. Otherwise, you risk sounding *salesy*. If you sound *salesy*, you lose credibility. You will know if you are sounding *salesy* by your prospects' expressions of skepticism and disbelief.

Use the negotiation strategies that work for you. Modify ones that don't, or use them to spur ideas for your negotiation strategy, or just don't use them. There are plenty of approaches to negotiating in the software sales process.

We don't discount

When prospects request a price concession, just say *no*.

Explain to prospects that your company has done the research. Your software is competitively priced for what it accomplishes; it is fair and reasonable.

It would be unfair to other customers if you lowered your price.

One of the reasons your software is so good is because your company invests in research and development. You are able to do that because you have profit to reinvest in your software so that it keeps improving. If you charged less, you would be like your competitors whose software is inferior.

If your prospect still demands a concession, negotiate a red herring or payment terms.

Red herrings

Include red herrings in your proposals. A red herring is something unimportant used to stop people from noticing or thinking about something important. So include unimportant *extras* in your proposal that prospects will likely negotiate at some point, like a fee for training, a fee for support after X hours of free support, or a fee for additional software modules. These *red herrings* distract your prospects from negotiating your base price.

Red herrings should be low cost, easy-to-throw-in services or modules. You can give away a red herring and prospects feel great, and your generosity has little or no impact on profit.

Negotiate terms, not money

Ask for aggressive payment terms. For example, require 60% upon approval of paperwork and 40% upon start of implementation. Or, one year paid in advance. Or, a support services fee due quarterly in advance. Or some other aggressive terms.

Payments terms are a form of a red herring. Your prospects will focus on negotiating payment terms instead of your software price.

Negotiation mindset

Your software is $100,000. Your prospect offers $80,000, which means you made an $80,000 sale. Now you just need to make a $20,000 sale.

The way you think about selling and negotiating matters. It's easier to make a $20,000 sale than a $100,000 sale. In this case, the fact that your prospect is willing to pay $80,000 means you're 80% of the way there!

Now only $20,000 is standing in the way of your prospect owning your software and receiving all the associated benefits.

Flinch

If a prospect says anything about your price being too high, flinch. For example, Mr. Prospect says, "Your software costs too much."

Salesperson replies, "Too *much*?" Then silence.

Mr. Prospect feels misguided for saying your software costs too much. He tends to feel obligated to justify why your software is too expensive.

Flinching is a way to begin a negotiation process that gives you an upper hand. It forces your prospect to justify his reasoning for a discount request.

Ask for more

If your list price is $50,000, ask for $55,000. Negotiate down to $50,000. Be sure to get management approval, of course!

Higher authority

Defer to a higher authority.

"Mr. Prospect, I appreciate your offer. I'll have to run this by my Vice President [higher authority] to see if there is any way we could approve selling at such a discount."

Using a higher authority enables you to regroup on your negotiating strategy. It also causes prospects to feel they are getting the best possible price since their discount request is being considered by management.

Prospects don't need the lowest price

Your prospects don't need the lowest price. They need to *feel* like they got the best possible price. Consider these two versions of a negotiation:

First version:

      Your software costs $50,000.

      Your prospect says, "We can only afford $40,000."

      You respond, "$49,000."

      Prospect says, "$41,000."

      You say, "Okay, $45,000, that's it."

      You win the sale.

Replay:

      Your software costs $50,000.

      Your prospect says, "We can only afford $40,000."

      You respond, "$49,000."

      Prospects says, "$41,000."

      You respond, "The best we can do is $48,500."

Prospect says, "Okay, $48,250, that's it."

In the first case, you sold your software for $45,000.

In the replay, you sold your software for $48,250. $3,250 bucks more.

In *both* cases, the prospect feels like he got the best price.

In the first case, you started with a $1,000 discount. Then you discounted another $4,000 to arrive at $45,000.

In the replay, you started with a $1,000 discount. Then you discounted another $500, then another $250, so your prospect feels like that's the most you can possibly discount.

In the first case, the amount of each successive discount *increased* in the negotiation process. In the replay, the amount of each discount *decreased* in the negotiation process.

Always use the replay method. As you offer discounts, start with a number that is a discount from the list price. If you have to negotiate further, offer an additional discount where the difference is smaller, not greater, than the first offer.

Your prospects need to *feel* like they got the best possible price. Make them feel that way. Offer discounts in decreasing amounts during the negotiation process, sell your software for the highest price, and make your prospects feel they got the best possible deal.

Present price discounts in writing

If you acquiesce to a price concession, put it in writing. When it's in writing, prospects believe *that's it*. They are not getting any more.

It is similar to how many hotels get guests to checkout on time. Hotel operators compared rooms with and without published checkout times. They concluded that checkout times in writing increased adherence.

When you present a discount in writing, it adds authority and firmness to your agreement.

There's something powerful about terms or conditions being *in writing* that makes us feel it's the rule and we have to abide by it!

It's not their money!

In business-to-business sales, prospects are trained to ask for price concessions. So they do. But remember, it's not *their* money they are spending. Yes, good employees are sensitive to spending their company's money. The fact that a purchasing team member *attempted* to negotiate the price is sometimes all the team is really interested in accomplishing. Now they can tell their management they tried to get a lower price.

"That's all that's in our budget"

When requesting a discount, prospects often say, "That's all that's in our budget."

So have a discussion about how the company (department) arrived at its budget. You need to be delicate during the conversation, but the bottom line is the budgeting process is flawed and sufficient funds for software were not allocated.

Now the conversation transitions to how funds can be reallocated to the software acquisition budget and away from discounting the selling price of your software.

Apologize to discount requests

When a prospect asks for a discount, apologize.

"Mr. Prospect, I apologize. I feel like I haven't done my job. Our software is worth every penny we charge for it. If you don't think it's worth it, I haven't explained our value proposition as well as I should have."

If give, get

Never make a concession without getting something in return. If you give something away, get something back. In return for acquiescing to a price concession, ask for something from your prospect.

For example, "Mr. Prospect, if I can get approval to offer this discount, will you agree to the following?

> *Provide a reference letter once we're up and running?*
>
> *Participate in our marketing survey?*
>
> *Refer me to a colleague?*
>
> *Attend the user conference?*
>
> *Be flexible on your go-live date?*
>
> *Participate in a case study?*
>
> *Take referral calls from other prospects?"*

It's quid pro quo!

Yes or yes decisions

Have prospects choose between yes and yes, versus yes and no.

For example, "Mr. Prospect, we can't approve your discount request, but we can either extend our terms or not charge for the _____ module. Which would you prefer?"

Now your prospect is not choosing between purchasing your software or not, she is choosing between ways to purchase your software!

Low cost is lower quality

Everyone inherently knows that items priced significantly lower than other similar items, usually have significantly lower quality. You pay more for higher quality.

If you're buying a desk, filing cabinet, reading lamp, coffee maker, or toaster, making your selection based on cost makes sense. Sure, you want quality, but you don't need to pay for the highest quality. You just need decent quality, something that will get the job done.

Buying software is entirely different than buying a desk, lamp, or toaster. You *need* the best. Unlike an uncomfortable desk or a toaster that takes too long, business application software is often the lifeblood of your company. There is no room for lower quality.

Have conversations about the quality of your software. There is a reason you have lower cost competitors. Their software is nowhere near the same quality as your software.

Remind your prospects of the common expressions, *you get what you pay for*, *let the buyer beware*, and *cheap pays twice*.

Help prospects realize that too much is at stake if they choose low quality software.

Software is an investment

Investment

"The outlay of money usually for income or profit: capital outlay…"

Merriam-Webster.com

When you discuss the business case for purchasing your software, refer to it as an investment. Talk about the long-term impact on business. You are simply asking for one check. The company will be getting year over year returns on your software (perhaps in the millions annually!). Your software does not cost too much when you look at it this way; it costs too little.

Notably less expensive competition

If you have competitors whose software costs notably less, there is a reason.

By notably, I mean the cost of their software is 30% (or more) less than the cost of your software. It's common for true competitors' software to be priced within 10% to 20% of each other. But when a competitor is notably less, there *has* to be a reason.

You must find and exploit the difference. You must be able to explain why your software is 30%+ more expensive.

Prospects need to understand why comparing your software to the discount-priced competitor's software is an apples to oranges comparison, not an apples to apples comparison. Although apples and oranges share a few similarities, both are fruit and round, that's where their likeness ends. You and your competitor both sell application software, but that's where the similarity stops.

The competitor's cost is low for a reason. Tell your prospects what that reason is.

The price is going up next quarter

If you tell prospects that the price of your software is going up, they will think twice about asking for a discount. In essence, they get a discount if they buy before the price increases.

"Mr. Prospect, there's no way I can give you a discount. The price of our software is going up next month."

Offer a discount before they ask

Similar, but not quite as effective as *the price is going up next quarter*, offer a discount for purchasing your software within a timeframe.

"Mr. Prospect, this special pricing is for this quarter only. It goes away next quarter."

While some prospects may be motivated to purchase, many will assume that if you can give a discount now, you can give a discount any time.

However, the strategy still causes prospects to think twice about asking for an even greater a discount.

Walk

Never hesitate to walk from a deal. There are only three possible outcomes.

Here's the first and best outcome. When you tell a prospect, "I'm sorry, that's the best we can do. I'll keep in touch with you in case anything changes," they acquiesce and buy at your *final offer*. When you are willing to walk, prospects feel they definitely got the lowest price they'll ever get.

The second outcome is that you walk. Then, after some internal strategy work, you call back in a day or so. You present a new, creative idea. Now, you are back at the negotiating table.

The third outcome is that you walk and it's over. You shake hands or hang up and update your CRM to closed lost status. You debrief with your sales manager, learn lessons, and move on. While obviously not ideal, you'll be better at your next negotiation.

What you can do today

- Review your cost justification presentation and determine which ROI strategies can be applied.
- Try your enhanced cost justification presentation.
- Refine it as needed based on your prospects' reactions.

Chapter 10. Demonstration close

<table>
<tr><td>**Executive summary**</td></tr>
</table>

One of these four actions will take place at the close of a software demonstration.

1. Prospects purchase
2. Prospects agree on a purchase action
3. Prospects say they will not buy
4. Prospects are still interested, but there is no action plan

Executed successfully, the close of your software demonstration should make your prospects feel uneasy about their status quo and enthused about your software's potential.

Chapter details include the following:

- A simple, surefire approach to the close of your demonstration, and how to agree on the end at the beginning.
- How to manage each of the four potential demonstration outcomes, including top producer stories.
- Tips on reading and reacting to prospects during the demonstration, setting up an expeditious and successful reference check plan, and enabling your prospects to sell internally on your behalf.

How to close your demonstration

The last five to ten minutes of your demonstration are *the close*. Executed successfully, *the close* should make your prospects feel uneasy about their status quo and enthused about your software's potential.

During this time do the following:

- Provide an executive summary of your software's value proposition
- Summarize the prospects' status quo (remind them of their challenges)
- If there are fewer than four people attending the demonstration, ask each person for his or her feedback; otherwise, solicit feedback from select purchasing team members
- Ask for a commitment to perform the next purchasing action

Four options upon close

Four things happen at the close of a software demonstration. These are the steps in order of preference:

1. Prospects purchase

2. A purchase action is agreed upon
3. Prospects say they will not buy
4. There is still interest, but no action plan

One: prospects purchase

Woohoo! Obviously the best option.

Get a credit card number, a purchase order, or a deposit check. Get paperwork approved. If prospects can't provide whatever it is that you need to finalize the deal, make sure you have a commitment to get it taken care of promptly.

Congratulate your prospects on their intelligent decision. Reassure them. Be excited for them. (Don't thank them. They should be thanking you.)

Manage expectations regarding the implementation plan.

Wrap up the conversation fast. Don't keep talking. If you do, you risk some other item coming up that could slow down the final steps. Get the order and go!

Get on with your next prospect.

Two: purchase action agreed upon

If your prospect commits to performing a purchasing action(s) within a timeframe, great! You are leading prospects efficiently through their purchasing process.

In pre-demonstration discovery, I discussed streamlining your prospects' purchasing process by exploring ways to perform actions in parallel, shorten time between actions, reduce the time it takes to perform an action, etc. This is a good time to revisit that conversation.

Immediately post demonstration, confirm who'll do what and by when via email.

Three: prospects say they will not buy

During one of my many early career lessons in how *not* to sell software, at the conclusion of my demonstration, a prospect said, "Thanks Brian, but we're not going to move forward."

I was discouraged. I had worked hard to get to the software demonstration stage. I had reasons to believe I would win the sale.

I debriefed with my sales manager, Rich Fuchs, a mentor. He let me lament. *Then*, he high-fived me!

I was confused. I had lost a deal.

Rich said, "Get to a *yes* or get to *no*. The *maybes* kill you."

He told me that *maybes* get stuck in your sales funnel. They clog it up. *Maybes* use up valuable sales minutes. The faster you can agree that this purchase makes sense, *or not*, the better!

Rich said, "*Maybes* make for small commission checks."

Since I wasn't clear on my prospect's reasoning for deciding not to purchase, Rich had me make a follow-up call. More on that in the post-demonstration activities section.

Four: still interested, no action plan

If, upon conclusion of your demonstration, prospects indicate that they are still interested, but are unwilling to commit to performing a purchasing action, you are stuck in the *maybe* category. The one that Rich said kills you.

However, sometimes there is no way around it. You have to conclude with a maybe. A key decision maker was not present. The participants are reluctant to express their thoughts. Budgets have been put on hold. An upcoming event prevents them from discussing the software purchase right away. And so on.

Learn what their plans are. Assume they have to talk amongst themselves. Inquire what information they need in order to decide whether or not to continue their purchasing process.

Ask about their timeline. When will they want to talk next? Send a calendar invite to confirm.

If you are stuck in a non-FILO situation, where you are unable to be the last to demonstrate your software, the prospects will need to see a competitor's demonstration before making any decision. When this happens, set traps for your competitor as we discussed earlier (e.g. give your prospects questions to ask your competitor).

Be helpful. Give them a software evaluation checklist. Provide a summary of your software's value proposition.

Ideally, your sales skills have influenced your prospects and created a mindset in which they are planning to purchase your software. They are looking at a competitor because they feel they have an obligation, not because they really have an interest in buying.

Agree on the end at the beginning

As part of your upfront contract, during the opening of your software demonstration gain agreement regarding what their next steps will be at the conclusion of the demonstration. If the demonstration validates that your prospect can achieve certain objectives, he will take the next purchasing action.

You are agreeing on the end at the beginning!

Now you can close with:

"Mr. Prospect, at the beginning of the demonstration, we agreed that if our software could solve [business challenges] _____, _____, and _____, it would make sense to continue your purchasing process."

"What are your thoughts?"

Note, it is important that you have this conversation with a sense of caring and concern. Be careful not to come across as aggressive or demanding.

Read and react to what's going on

At the close of a demonstration, prospects are sometimes reluctant to tell you how they feel. Purchasing team members want to speak with each other before opening up to you.

When this happens, you can still get a read regarding what's going on in their minds by watching for *tells*.

A *tell* is an expression used by poker players. It is when a player's behavior or demeanor provides clues to that player's assessment of his hand. Good poker players don't exhibit *tells*.

Fortunately, most prospects would not make good poker players. When purchasing team members like your software, they exhibit *tells*.

Listen not only to what they say regarding your software, but to how they say it. When people are enthused, you can hear it in their voice. However, sighs or long pauses indicate that they are facing a tough decision.

If demonstrating in-person, observe purchasing team members' physical expressions and how they interact with each other. You can tell whether they are excited or cautious.

By watching for *tells*, you will often be able to determine whether purchasing team members are leaning towards a yes or no decision.

If it appears prospects are leaning towards a *yes* decision, maintain momentum and gain commitment to their final purchasing actions.

If it appears prospects are leaning towards a *no* decision, follow up and engage in conversation. Ask questions to understand their current thinking. Enable your prospects to reach a yes decision by revisiting your software's unique value proposition. Provide new, additional information regarding your software's value proposition.

Read and react to what's going on during your demonstration. Watch for *tells*. Respond accordingly.

Makes good business sense

During your *closing argument* you need your prospects to feel that purchasing your software makes plain old good business sense. Remind them that even though there are many things they could spend money on, your software is an obvious priority. It just makes sense!

Reference check plan

Reference checks are when prospects speak with existing customers regarding their experience with your company's software and support. Reference checks are common when selling costly or complex business application software that is used by multiple people.

Do not underestimate the value and importance of reference checks. Prospects often weigh them heavily. I have performed many win/loss analyses for software companies. I've commonly heard customers say that reference checks pushed purchasing team members over the edge (one way or the other) regarding their decision.

Make it final final

If performing a reference check is a final step, ask your prospect to approve paperwork, *subject to* a successful reference check. Make it their final, final step. They are buying your software, but they need to speak with references as a last step.

If this is not feasible, either because your company legally cannot or because your customer simply will not, learn what your prospects intend to do post reference check. If possible, when providing the references, schedule a date for a follow-up conversation.

Make it easy

Make it easy for prospects to make reference checks (either phone conversations or site visits) by coordinating schedules. Ask your prospect for timeslots he has available to perform reference checks. Then, coordinate a time with your established customer to have a conversation with your new prospect.

Make it easy for your customer to be a reference. Tell your customer what your new prospect's likely areas of interest will be. Ask your customer to talk about specific features and benefits that you know your prospect has an interested in.

Your customers and prospects will appreciate your making it easy to connect.

Competitive advantage

Ideally, you will have commitment from your prospects that they intend to purchase, assuming they like what they hear from your references. However, some prospects will need to speak with your references *and* your competitor's references before making a purchase decision.

Make reference checking your competitive advantage. Select customers who considered purchasing from your competitor, or even better, switched from your competitor's software to yours.

Ask your customer to speak about how he selected your software over a competitor who was also in the running.

Reference check timing

The sooner you can coordinate reference checking post demonstration, the better. Every day that passes post demonstration, you are at risk that the purchase of your software will be delayed because of some new business priority.

By moving quickly to coordinate reference checks, particularly if your competition doesn't, prospects have a good perception of your company. They think, if this company has this many customers ready and willing to give references, they must have happy customers.

Make reference checking happen as soon as possible after your software demonstrations.

Reference check prioritization

Prospects request multiple references, but often speak with just one.

Prospects just don't have time to speak with everyone. If the first reference they speak to is a contagiously-enthusiastic raving fan, who articulates the business value of your software, your prospects will not feel the need to speak with other references.

You will have accelerated your sales process.

Select "select" references

Carefully select your references. You need them to endorse your software for the right reasons.

Regarding titles, likes want to talk with likes, meaning a CFO wants to talk to a CFO; a VP Sales wants to talk to a VP Sales, etc.

Regarding situations, match them. If a prospect wants rapid installation, connect him with a customer who experienced a rapid installation. If ongoing support is of utmost importance to your prospect, connect her with a customer who is enthusiastic about your company's support.

Regarding communication styles, select your references so their styles work for each other. Have detail-oriented prospects speak with detail-oriented customers. Have friendly conversationalists speak with friendly conversationalists.

Regarding all references, select those who are excited about your software. If your competitors' references are matter-of-fact and yours are enthusiastic, the result will be a fat commission check for you.

Thank customers profusely

Show appreciation for your customer who takes time from her busy day to chat with your prospect. Send a handwritten thank-you note. Send a gift. Take them to lunch. Let them know that you appreciate their taking the time to deliver a positive reference.

Let customers know what happened

Let your references know the outcome. It's a simple courtesy, often overlooked. People like to know how the story ended... especially when they played a part in it.

Make sure demo participants are prepared to sell internally

I've discussed internal selling, where your prospect has to persuade others in the company that purchasing your software is an affordable priority.

For example, a CFO, an attorney, or an IT Director may never use the software you are selling, so they have no reason to attend a demonstration. However, if they are a purchasing team member, they definitely have a say as to whether it is purchased.

Remind your demonstration participants to internally sell and give them the tools they need to do it!

The tools can be a compilation of ideas I've discussed throughout this book. A competitive analysis chart, a decision-criteria-ranking-form, an endorsement by the press, a self-administrable slide presentation, an ROI presentation, etc.

Don't assume that they have the tools they need. Before sending them on their way, ask them if there's anything you can furnish to help them inform decision makers who were unable to attend.

A recorded demonstration doesn't work

I can't tell you how many times I've heard this *brilliant* (stupid) idea. *Let's have prospects watch a prerecorded software demonstration!*

This harkens back to the days of the video cassette recorder (VCR). Marketers were so excited about *sending a video!* The belief was that you could send prospects a VCR via mail (snail was all they had back then) and that prospects would actually plug it in and watch it. They don't.

They don't click links and watch software demonstrations online either.

I've said it before, but I'll restate it: executives are busy, very busy.

Prerecorded software demonstrations don't work. However, *brief* videos that entice prospects to want to see a demonstration work fine. If you are going to leverage video in your software marketing and sales process, use it as a tool to persuade prospects to see a demonstration.

Close early and delight your prospect

I've never met a businessperson who exclaimed when a meeting concluded early, "Hold on. This meeting isn't supposed to end for another 15 minutes!"

However, I have observed many businesspeople glance at watches and start fidgeting as soon as a meeting goes into overtime.

Conclude your software demonstrations a few minutes earlier than expected. Prospects will appreciate it.

What you can do today

- Pre-plan the close of your next software demonstration. What are your prospects' next steps in their purchasing process? How can you expedite their next steps?
- How will you handle each of the four potential outcomes (prospects purchase, prospects agree on a purchase action, prospects say they will not buy, prospects are still interested, but there is no action plan)?

Part Three – Post demonstration

Chapter 11. You can win or lose post-demo

Executive summary

• Your post demonstration follow-up activities can influence your prospect's decision to purchase, or not.
• Post demonstration factors that can favorably influence your prospects include speed of follow-up, design and quality of your proposal, reference checking, and relevance and usefulness of the information you send.
 	
Chapter details include the following:
 	
   o Success stories of top producers' post demonstration follow-up activities, including what they do and how they do it.
   o Specific plans for post demonstration activities that will enable you to win more sales.
   o How to use your prospects' time wisely (so your competitor's can't).

Give prospects what they need post-demo

Janice Houston sells quality management software to the life sciences industry. She is a top producer.

Her software is a suite of solutions specially engineered for the life sciences. It helps with patient safety, audit tracking, electronic reporting, workflows, and software validation requirements for regulatory bodies. It is based on current ISO quality management standards, and it serves as a central repository for simplified reporting.

The majority of Janice's purchasing team members are scientists and engineers. They are detail oriented. They make careful decisions. They are deliberate and unhurried.

They rarely make a purchase decision upon conclusion of a demonstration. They need time to contemplate and discuss their decision.

Janice said, "I believe that I win the sale after my software demonstration." She explained that while a niche market, life sciences is highly competitive. "I have a comprehensive follow-up process that I adhere to." She sends custom emails (modified templates) that include detailed and relevant information regarding her software.

She said, "I call it the backstory of our software. My purchasing team members relish details and data, so I give it to them."

She has had more than one new customer tell her that the follow-up information had a positive impact on her purchase decision.

Determine what information, and in what format, your prospects need post-demo. Give it to them.

Use your prospect's time wisely (so your competitors can't)

Mechanical engineers use computer aided design software (CAD). They also need metal prototype parts so they can experiment with different product designs.

Jennie Stewart sells software that interconnects CAD software with the nuances of prototype design. She has always achieved or exceeded quota.

To use Jennie's software, engineers have to do a bit of pre-work. Jennie explained that data needs to be converted, then imported. Business processes need to be refined. Application program interfaces need to be revised. IT needs to validate security measures, and training needs to be scheduled.

> I use my prospect's time wisely. I persuade them to start the preliminary implementation process necessary to use software like mine. Since I take control and lead them through the process, they are interacting with me more than they are interacting with my competitors. Mechanical Engineers only have so many minutes in a day to discuss software configuration. I get them to spend those minutes with me, which causes them to be more comfortable purchasing software from me than from my competitors.

Use your prospect's time wisely. The more time they spend interacting with you, the less time they have to spend with your competitor.

Follow up fast

Whatever the follow-up plan, do it fast.

Imagine you are your prospect. After the demonstration wrap-up, you (the prospect) attend a few other meetings. Back at your desk, you check your email. The salesperson's promised follow-up information is waiting for you in your Inbox, and he's thoughtfully included even more. You hadn't expected to receive the information until the following day.

Do you think that makes a favorable impression? It does – particularly if your competitor follows up in the usual way, and doesn't send the promised follow-up information for another day or two!

The speed of your post demonstration follow-up can give you a competitive advantage.

Proposal quality

During a post-sale debrief with a new customer, I was shown three proposals from three different companies. The customer said, "Which looks like the best company to you?"

The proposals were laid out on a conference table.

"Don't read them, just pick them up and peruse them," he said.

One proposal stood out instantly. It was cover bound. The paper was high quality. It had tabs that made for easy reading. Inside, the pages had color graphics. The format enabled me to quickly scan and understand the information.

The other competitors' proposals were simply inferior by comparison.

Send high quality follow-up information.

Proposal design

Tim Edsley, a top producer, sells software to manage merchants' credit card payment processing. This software manages the interactions between the credit card issuer, card holder, merchant, submitter, acquirer, and the interchange network. It also facilitates the chargeback process. It's complex.

Tim designs his proposals so they simplify the complexity of his software. Tim said, "I include graphics and color coded process flows. I make it easy to understand multiple and complex work flows."

His proposals also include an executive summary, a detailed overview, and an extended comprehensive overview. Tim says, "I'll even send the infinitesimal details, if that's what you need."

Tim believes that the design of his proposals is a distinguishing factor that enables him to win more deals.

Handwritten notes

Think about how you feel when you check your snail mail and see a handwritten envelop. You want to open it. You are curious. It's a break from the usual bills and junk mail.

Post demonstration, send handwritten notes to your prospects. It distinguishes you from your competition. Prospects appreciate a handwritten note.

You may be thinking, "Good idea, but who has time for that?"

It's true; the handwriting process will take an investment of time. If you keep each note short and stamps and stationery at the ready, the process can be streamlined.

You'll find it worth the time

Email templates

Make your follow-up email quick and easy. Use templates.

Depending on your situation, work with marketing or develop your own email templates.

It takes an investment of time to set up automated activities, but, as one top producer put it, "It's 'one and done'." You do the task once; you never do it again.

Here's a best practice checklist to assist with the design of your email templates.

- Does the subject line compel the recipient to *want* to read the email?
- Have you carefully considered to whom the email is addressed?
- Is your email scannable, containing subheads, bulleted lists, and bolded words?
- Does your first line compel the recipient to want to keep reading?
- Have you included "what's in it for them"?
- Do you have a clear call to action?
- Is there a benefit to your prospect to perform your call to action?
- Are you using formatting to highlight key points?
- Does your signature include relevant contact information?
- Have you used a postscript to drive home an important point?
- Can it be easily read on a mobile device?
- Is it easy for the recipient to reply with a short answer?

Update your CRM

For most tech sales pros, this is not easy or fun. But they do it.

Immediately post demonstration, update your CRM. Make notes so you can easily view a summary of the demonstration and your anticipated next steps. Assign follow-up dates.

Whether the demonstration ended with your winning or your losing the sale, document the reasons why.

The next time anyone brings up the prospect record, it should be easy to view a snapshot of the opportunity status.

Facetime

There's a reason the President of the United States flies around the world in Airforce One. Facetime.

Subject to the price range of your software and proximity to your prospect's location, visit your prospects post demonstration.

Meeting someone face-to-face develops a level of communication that simply can't be established any other way. Phone calls or video conferences are not the same.

Face-to-face meetings establish rapport and trust in a manner that simply can't be achieved otherwise.

Celebrate success, drown sorrow

Go out with your team after work. Celebrate your success or drown your sorrow.

Selling software is not easy. It helps to share sales stories with your peers.

Meeting for an appetizer, a soft drink, a beer, a martini (or some combination!) after work is a great way to debrief your software demonstration – and make your next one even better.

Expectation management after the close

When a prospect decides to purchase your software, manage her expectations and move to the next steps quickly. The time between your prospect verbally stating she intends to buy, and actually approving paperwork and preparing a deposit check is important.

When competitors get the word, they may not give up. They could swoop in with the big guns and make price concessions or offer additional modules or services at no charge. Also, buyer's remorse can creep in and cause your prospect to think twice about their decision.

So maintain momentum! Get a signature, a credit card, a check, or whatever signoff is needed to finalize the transaction.

Introduce your implementation and support team members to your customer. Be clear what the next steps will be. Tell your customer what your team will do and tell the team what they need to do.

Let the team know you're standing by should they need you, but avoid remaining involved post sale, unless your position description calls for you to perform post sale support activities. It's time to close the next deal!

What you can do today

- Lay out a plan for what you will do post *your next* demonstration.
- Follow your plan.
- Refine and streamline your plan as you assess results.

Chapter 12. Post demonstration debrief

Executive summary

- Always perform a post demonstration debrief. It can be done efficiently, and it enables you to deliver a better demonstration the next time.
- Your demonstration debrief session agenda includes a short discussion about these three questions:
  1. What worked?
  2. What could you have done better?
  3. What can you do now? (It's not too late!)

Chapter details include the following:

  o How to lay out a post demonstration plan that can determine the difference between winning and losing the sale.
  o How to perform an efficient and effective post demonstration debrief, and how not to get a demerit from Marketing.
  o An important note to management.

Demonstration debrief session

Most lucrative occupations require that you pay to learn about the profession. If you are a doctor, for example, and you want to become a surgeon, you have to pay to go back to school. To become a real estate broker or an attorney, you need to pay for extensive testing and certification. Financial advisors have to pay to be accredited.

To the contrary, salespeople *get paid* to learn. We learn every time we deliver a demonstration. Every software demonstration can get better based on our experience from the previous demonstration. This is why it's so important to perform a demonstration debrief as soon as possible post demonstration.

Demo debriefs take just five minutes and they have a dramatic effect on your demonstration-to-close ratio.

Ideally, debrief with a peer or sales manager who participated in or observed your demonstration. Worst case, self-debrief!

Think through your sales process, from pre-demonstration planning to the close of your demonstration. Ask three simple questions:

1. What worked?

> What were the highlights? When were prospects most engaged? What conversations were most effective? What should you do in your next demonstration because it worked so well in this demonstration?

2. What could you have done better?

What didn't go so well? When did prospects seem distant? Did you say anything that was poorly worded, or that they didn't understand? What should you not do in your next demonstration because it didn't go so well in this demonstration?

3. What can you do now? It's not too late!

Unlike that surgeon I talked about earlier, salespeople can always go back to the prospect. If a surgeon loses his scalpel, it's not so easy to open the patient up again. If a salesperson thinks of something she should have said or done, in many cases, she still can. You can call or email your prospect and let them know whatever it was you meant to tell them, but forgot. Determine if, as a result of your demo debrief, you have reason to reach back out to your prospect.

Build your demo debrief into your calendar. Upon close of your demonstration, don't check email or return a call. Invest just five minutes; that's all it takes to perform a post demonstration debrief.

What does Marketing need?

Your marketing team can learn from your demonstration as well. Marketing can develop better tools to help you sell, but only *if* they hear about your demonstration experience.

Ask your marketing team what it needs and give it to them. Again, five minutes is all it takes. So now you are up to 10 minutes of post demonstration activities, or less. Post demo debriefs get faster and more valuable the more often you perform them.

Some marketing teams set up CRM questions to be answered post demonstration. In order to move a prospect from the demo stage to the proposal stage, for example, you are asked to respond to some questions. Or, if you move a prospect to a *closed-lost* stage, you are asked to check a box as to why the sale was lost.

Other marketing teams are less formal. A verbal debrief or email summary may be just fine.

Find out what information your marketing team needs post demonstration and develop a process for giving it to them.

How not to get a demerit from Marketing

When planning your software demonstration, integrate your website's content into it.

Marketing teams spend time and money understanding your software's target market, value proposition, and competitive advantages. Don't reinvent your marketing message. Use it.

During your post demo debrief, let the marketing team know what resonated with prospects and what didn't. You'll get a merit, not a demerit!

Note to management, do you really have a sales problem?

I want to meet the proverbial salesperson who can sell ice to Eskimos!

Eskimos simply don't need ice.

Likewise, some software simply isn't as sellable as everyone anticipates it will be. It really is like trying to sell ice to Eskimos.

If you fine-tune your software demonstration and you are still not closing enough sales, perhaps you need to rework your software or your go-to-market strategy. Or, perhaps you need to recognize there is not a market for your software.

For example:

Software for management of global travel. While it was feature/functionality rich, there were just not enough reasons to change and unseat incumbents. Marketing could not develop a message that caused prospects to express an interest.

Software that Google started giving away. It couldn't be sold. There was no longer a market for the software.

Software for the design and administration of sales compensation plans. The value proposition wasn't great enough for small companies and the software wasn't designed for large companies. It couldn't be sold until it was reworked to handle large companies.

Software to manage unused, outdated IT inventory, like old monitors and printers. It was cool stuff with more functionality than Excel, but ultimately Excel accomplished the same thing just fine. It couldn't be sold.

Venture Capitalists have endless stories of software companies that couldn't get sales traction. Sometimes failure to sell software is not due to ineffective sales efforts. Sometimes it can't be sold.

If you apply the software demonstration strategies in this book and you're still not closing enough deals, you may be trying to sell ice to Eskimos.

What you can do today

- Schedule a ten-minute post demonstration debrief after your next demonstration.
- Evaluate what worked, what you could have done better, and what you can do now.
- Using this discipline, continually improve your next software demonstration.

Part Four – Best Practices of Top Producers

I've had the privilege of speaking with numerous top producing software sales professionals about how and why they are successful. Not everything I've learned fits in the process outlined above.

Here are additional best practices for selling software.

Does your software require ongoing internal support?

Application software sometimes requires that your prospects have employees who are available and capable to provide ongoing support.

For example, if you sell software that requires ongoing website changes for product descriptions, your prospect needs to employ a Merchandiser.

If you sell software that requires an internal administrator to be available 24/7, your prospect may need to employ another IT person.

If you sell software that manages inbound marketing, your prospect will need an employee to monitor social media conversations and reply if necessary.

Your software can't solve prospects' pressing business challenges without the team members to support it!

Jim Swenson, a top producer who sells sales enablement software explained his success, "My prospects either have sales operations support team members available to support our software on an ongoing basis, or they don't. For my software to work correctly it requires that prospects employ a full time sales operations person. Depending on the situation, I sell differently."

Sales enablement software puts information that salespeople need in their hands when they need it, in a way they can use it. The information is dynamic. In fact, the more a customer uses sales enablement software, the better the information becomes. But this can't happen if no one is interpreting dashboards regarding use of the information, or no one has ownership of keeping sales enablement software up-to-date.

Jim told me that if a prospect needs to hire sales operations support people, she wants to know:

- What are the job descriptions?
- What are the qualifications a candidate will need?
- How do I find candidates to interview?
- How do I know if candidates should be given an offer?
- How much payroll cost will I incur?
- How long will it take me to get someone up-to-speed to support your software?

Prospects, who already have sales operations resources, want to know:

- How exactly is sales operations involved?

- How much time does sales operations need to allocate overall?
- What skills does the sales operations support team require?
- How does the team acquire those skills?
- How do we keep the team updated on those skills? How much will it cost?

Jim said, "It's a sales process within my sales process. Even if the CEO and the VP of Sales want to move forward with a purchase decision, it can't happen if there isn't a sales operations function ready to go. So I answer those questions, whether they ask them or not!"

When Jim is performing his pre-demonstration discovery, he told me, "When I'm determining if prospects are a reasonable match to my top-tier prospect definition, I always have conversations regarding their willingness and ability to allocate existing resources or to hire those resources. If their answer is *no* to both questions, I move on. They will not be able to get value from my software."

Your software can't solve your prospects' business challenges if they don't have internal resources for ongoing internal support. Show them how to get the resources they'll need.

Pendulum theory

An opportunity is like a pendulum in motion. It swings to one side, then the other side. During the software sales process, sales opportunities are always in motion. Prospects are always swinging from one side to the other. They decide to purchase your software, or not.

If a prospect is on the not purchase side after your software demonstration, you need to swing the pendulum back to purchase. It's okay if they are on the not purchase side. There is only one way their pendulum can swing!

If a prospect is on the purchase side after your software demonstration, you need to keep the pendulum where it is; get your prospect to approve the purchase of your software.

Use verbal communication that engages

Have you ever listened to a monotone presenter? A vanilla one-flavor-fits-all voice is boring. It turns people off. However, a presenter who uses vocal variety is appealing.

Have you ever listened to a presenter who did not articulate clearly? Stating words incorrectly or incoherently makes a presenter seem unprofessional. However, a presenter who articulates clearly has an aura of professionalism.

Dawn Shelton is a top producer who learned about the importance of using vocal variety and articulating clearly in an interesting way. A top producer, Dawn sells subscription management software to libraries. Her purchasing team members are intellectual; most are librarians.

Dawn flew to Denver to give a demonstration. Her flight back home was the following morning. Her prospect invited her for a backyard barbeque with the team.

Dawn told me, "After some tasty barbeque, they broke out a colossal dictionary. I've never seen one so large. We played a word game that required referencing the dictionary."

Her purchasing team members were articulate in every way. During the game, Dawn learned quickly that diction and enunciation were as important to librarians as the written word.

To make sure she was communicating appropriately with her purchasing team members, Dawn worked with speech coach, Sybil Tonkonogy. Sybil observed one of Dawn's software demonstrations. During her debrief, Sybil said, "Dawn, you have amazing software and you do a great job showing its features and benefits and overall value proposition. However, we need to work on your articulation and vocal variety."

Dawn worked with Sybil for a number of coaching sessions. They recorded and listened to Dawn reading different sentences. Sybil assigned voice exercises. Dawn did her assignments and started making changes to how she spoke when she demonstrated her software.

Dawn told me that she stopped dropping her T's. She stopped gasping in mid-sentence. She varied her pace and volume. And she articulated more clearly.

Dawn said, "What I learned from working with Sybil, I'll use forever, in life and business. My demonstrations improved dramatically. Prospects are more engaged since I became a better communicator."

Articulate clearly

My Mom was a phone operator in the early days of landlines. To make a phone call, you would speak with the operator and ask her (all operators were female in those days) to dial a phone number. In order to make sure she didn't call a wrong number, the operator would repeat back the phone number before dialing. All operators went through training to articulate properly.

Mom told me that she was trained to say one as *wuhn*, two as *too*, three as *thahree*, four as *fohr*, five as *fahyv*, six as *siks*, seven as *sev-uhn*, eight as *eyt*, nine as *nahyn*. All operators had to articulate numbers consistently and clearly. They literally had to pass a speech exam during their training.

The result was that no matter which operator answered, the customers' experience was the same. Before an operator dialed a number, it was verified. Customers confirmed or corrected the number. Rarely did an operator dial a wrong number and customers enjoyed a consistent experience.

During your software demonstrations, the same lessons apply. You don't necessarily have to state nine as *nahyn,* but be sure to articulate clearly, so you communicate more effectively.

Voice exercises

Fine-tune your verbal communication. Try these voice exercises.

Project your voice

Project. Hit the back of the room with your voice. Breathe deeply, look to the back of the room, and push your voice there.

Similar to the smart habit of keeping the gas tank in your car above half full, breathe deeply and fill your lungs as you speak. Don't gasp for air.

Speak with the emotional authenticity

Speech Coach Susan Dugdale suggests using *the ham sandwich* exercise. Repeat the words *ham sandwich* in as many varying ways as you can.

For example, say it angrily, happily, sadly, lovingly, despairingly, laughingly, importantly, slyly, snidely, and shyly.

Learn to speak with emotional authenticity.

Learn from news reporters

Listen carefully to news reporters on TV and radio. Note how clearly they articulate. They hit their T's and D's. Every letter in a word is expressed clearly. They pause when appropriate. Their diction is perfect. Emulate news reporters!

Practice good posture

Sit with a straight back. Stand with your knees slightly bent and your weight on the balls of your feet. Correct posture improves your verbal communication.

Vary speed and volume

Vary how fast or slowly you speak. Raise or lower your voice.

Use pregnant pauses or speak a word slowly and softly. Then speak faster or louder.

Use variations of vocal speed and volume to emphasize certain points and communicate more effectively overall.

Don't be Charlie Brown's teachers or parents

During Charlie Brown (a renowned cartoon character) TV shows, when Charlie talks to Lucy, Linus, Pigpen, his classmates, or his friends, you can clearly understand what he is saying. When you hear a teacher or parent's voice, it sounds like, "Wah, wah, wah. Wah, wah, wha. Wha, wha, wha..."

The voices are flat and monotonous. It is painful to listen to.

Make sure you never sound like Charlie's teachers or parents.

Superfluous words

When listening to a recording of himself delivering a demonstration to a top-tier prospect, Gary Strauss counted the number of times he said, "Right?"

He told me, "It was so many; the number is not for publication."

Gary had no idea he used the word *right* so often. He felt embarrassed. He stopped saying the word. Gary said, "It took discipline. I had to wean myself off the word!"

Uhm, ah, right, ya know, wow, to be honest, really, awesome, and *like* are superfluous. "Like, ya know," don't use these words! Record and listen to yourself to make sure you aren't saying superfluous words, or worse, like Gary, saying them repeatedly.

Call out Tahiti breakers

If a purchasing team member has been silent during your remote or in-person demonstration, ask for her input. She may be engaged in your presentation, or she might be on what I refer to as a Tahiti break.

A Tahiti break means the prospect is not paying attention to your demonstration, so I assume she is thinking about being in Tahiti!

To make sure prospects are still attentive, ask questions of suspected Tahiti breakers. "Bill, do you think this process will work?" "Mary, how do you feel about this dashboard?" "Jim, will this work for your team?"

If they are engaged, they will have answers. If they're not engaged, you'll bring them back into the fold (and out of Tahiti!).

Your job starts when prospects say *No!*

If all your prospects watched a self-demo on the web, clicked a credit card, and started using your software, your company wouldn't need salespeople.

If your software had the lowest cost with the best functionality, your company wouldn't need salespeople, it would need demonstrators.

If you were a CEO and could run your company with no cost of sales (e.g. salespeople), wouldn't you do it?

That's why sales professionals like you are needed. No software is perfect and most software companies have competitors.

During your demonstrations, when prospects express objections or skepticism, think, *Okay, game on. Time to do my job.*

It's imperative that you are prepared to respond to every known objection. You either need to persuade your prospect your software is still the best solution or mutually agree that your software isn't appropriate.

As sales professionals, we are always looking in the mirror and saying, "What could I have done differently in order to win that sale?" Your software will never have the lowest cost and the most functionality. That's why you earn the big bucks!

Don't work on too many prospects at a time

If you work with too many prospects who are at the software demonstration stage of their purchasing process, you'll do a mediocre job with all of them. If you work with the right number of prospects, you can do an extraordinary job with all of them. You work less, but close more.

I've met top producers who sold multimillion dollar software. They could realistically work with three or four prospects at a time who were at the demo stage.

I've met top producers who sold low cost point solutions. They could realistically deliver five on-line demonstrations a day.

The number of prospects you can work at one time is limited. Know your limits.

Speak in prospects' time zones

Make it easy for prospects; communicate in their time zone.

For example, if you are located in Boston and you want to schedule a demonstration with a prospect on the west coast at 4:00pm, ask your prospect about their availability at 1:00pm. Allocate for the three-hour time zone difference.

The further away the prospect, the more important this adjustment becomes. For example, translating time zones between NY and Australia isn't a quick calculation prospects can do in their head; it's a 14-hour difference!

When software glitches happen

Picture yourself in your prospect's seat. You are watching a software demonstration and the system locks up. The salesperson can react in a couple of ways...

Reaction one:

"Oh, uh… hold on a minute. This doesn't usually happen. It must be the demo system. I'll, uh, see if rebooting helps and call our 800 number."

Reaction two:

"Let me demonstrate what you will do should this ever happen to you." The salesperson dials a number on speakerphone, and is greeted with, *"Hello Jim, Sarah in support here. I see your system is locked. I'm taking care of it right now because I know you are in a demonstration with Alcoa Tech. That was our security alerting us for unknown users. When you entered your title as an Alcoa Tech Vice President, we received a security notice. You'll be good to go in one minute."*

Okay, maybe your company's support is not as smooth as Jim's, but you are always given a choice: you can respond to software glitches with panic or with professionalism.

Even masters of technology demonstrations like the late Steve Jobs, CEO of Apple, occasionally run into a glitch. What made him a master is that it never rattled him.

If you receive an error message while demonstrating software, use it as an opportunity to discuss the benefits of your company's support program. If you respond with a deer-in-the-headlights look, your prospect won't feel confident about purchasing your software!

No commission for 2nd place

Wouldn't it be great if we received 50% of our commission check for coming in second place? Or how about 25% for making their shortlist?

As the saying goes, close only counts in horseshoes and hand grenades. In software sales, you either win the sale or lose the sale. Top producers know that "You came in second" or "You made the short list" means nothing.

No software is perfect

No business application software is perfect. At least, of the hundreds of software companies I've consulted with, none have ever had zero enhancements on their application development list.

Software can always be improved, but we still have to sell it as is.

Early in my career, during our weekly coaching session, my sales manager and mentor, Steve Swantek, was debriefing me about a sale I had lost. He asked me why I thought I lost the sale.

"Steve, our software needs to integrate with accounting. Between the lack of accounting integration and our competitors all offering 24/7 service, I couldn't compete," I explained.

"Anything else?" Steve asked.

"Yeah, marketing needs to give us a better feature comparison chart. We don't even list all of the features we have."

Steve was a great coach. He told me to "look in the mirror" and ask, "What could I have done to win that sale?"

Steve taught me to take responsibility. We talked through the lost deal.

I identified two features our software offered that our competitors didn't. I could easily present why the benefits of those features outweighed the benefits of accounting integration.

I came up with a positioning statement about how our customers don't need 24/7 support because our software is rock solid and our self-help screens are intuitive.

We looked at our feature comparison chart and drafted the additions we thought it needed. Steve said he'd run it by the Marketing Director for approval.

By looking in the mirror and taking responsibility for losing the sale, I came up with competitive positioning strategies that I used during my next software demonstration. After a little trial and error, I stopped losing sales to accounting integration, lack of 24/7 support, or feature lists.

Steve is the person who helped me understand it's up to me to win. He's the one who told me, "You're not getting a commission for second place."

Competitively positioning your software is your job.

Demonstration evaluation form

Record your demonstration, re-watch it, and evaluate it. It will be a learning experience.

You don't need to record every demonstration. Just a few select demonstrations each month or each quarter is enough to learn some valuable lessons.

Use this generic software demonstration evaluation form, or a hybrid that better matches your selling situation, to evaluate your demonstration after watching your video.

Software Demonstration Evaluation

(Example, create your own)

Prospect: _____

	Needs improvement	Satisfactory	Excellent
Planning			
Know *all* the purchasing team members	☐	☐	☐
Know *all* the needs (business problems to solve)	☐	☐	☐
Know the purchasing process	☐	☐	☐
Know where they are in the purchasing process	☐	☐	☐
Opening			
WIIFM (What's in it for my prospect?)	☐	☐	☐
Qualifications of team	☐	☐	☐
Agenda	☐	☐	☐
Time frame	☐	☐	☐
Additions to agenda	☐	☐	☐
Agreement on next step	☐	☐	☐
Body			
Memorable manner	☐	☐	☐
How software solves business problems	☐	☐	☐
Report usage	☐	☐	☐
Competitive knock-offs	☐	☐	☐
ROI analysis	☐	☐	☐
How to get started	☐	☐	☐
Close			
Life without solutions	☐	☐	☐
Agreement on next step & time frame	☐	☐	☐
Delivery			
Body language	☐	☐	☐
Success stories	☐	☐	☐
Vocal variety	☐	☐	☐
Visual aids	☐	☐	☐
Audience participation	☐	☐	☐
Completed within time limit	☐	☐	☐

Email for mobile devices, always

Assume all email correspondence is being received on a mobile device. Make it simple for prospects to read.

If you have attachments, summarize them in your email. Assume prospects don't have time or ability to retrieve and/or read attachments.

Use prospect's data

Dean Whittier is a top producer who sells software to manage steel mills.

Asked about his success, Dean said,

> I always enter my prospects' data in advance of the demonstration. Steel mills can manufacture a range of alloy elements, like manganese, nickel, chromium, molybdenum, boron, titanium, vanadium, tungsten, cobalt, and niobium. And those are just the common ones. I've had prospects that work with phosphorus, sulfur, silicon, nitrogen, and copper.

Dean explained that it took him about 20 to 30 minutes to enter his prospects' data pre-demonstration. He asks for examples of their alloy elements, and names of a few customers and suppliers. He even requests copies of a few recent purchase orders.

"When I demonstrate our software, it comes alive for them. They see their customers' names. They see their alloys. And when I show them how our software intakes a purchase order that is familiar to them, they love it!"

Examples of prospects' data to consider entering into your software pre-demo include the following:

- Customers' names
- Vendors' names
- Employees' names
- Product descriptions
- Part numbers
- Pricing by SKU, customer type, product type, etc.
- Commonly used forms

If you invest the time to enter prospects' data before your demonstration, it will be easier for prospects to identify how your software solves their challenges.

Professionals sell externally *and* internally

Sales pros always take responsibility for innovating ways to make the sale and reaching their sales goals, even in the face of common objections. However, there are circumstances when even the pros feel they have exhausted all options and keep losing to a common objection. This is the point where some internal selling may be required.

For example, if you feel you are losing sales because a feature set is lackluster (or lacking!), take responsibility for getting that feature set on your company's product development roadmap.

If you feel you are losing sales because a team member or department is not pulling its weight in the sales process, address the issue directly with that team member or with management (be sure to document your issue first).

If you feel you are losing sales because you don't have enough qualified sales leads, even though you've been generating as many leads as you can on your own, work with your marketing team to refine your lead generation or qualification strategy. Pointing a finger and blaming marketing only makes you look bad. Be part of the solution.

As a sales professional, *you* own winning or losing. It's easy to say, "I would have won if only we had that feature set, a better price strategy, faster implementation, etc." Instead, say, "I'm going to do some internal selling so I'll be able to offer that feature set, price strategy, implementation plan, etc."

I met a software sales pro who, upon losing to a particular competitor too often regarding the cost of data conversion, presented a data conversion pricing strategy to his finance team that was competitive, but still profitable. The finance team was happy to adopt it.

A software sales pro I know was tired of being beaten by a competitor with a product feature set that prospects preferred. He made his case to the product development team and that feature set was reprioritized.

When you lose a sale, the list of should haves and could haves is long, but *you* own it; no one else does.

When all else fails

If you get the dreaded call or email informing you that your prospect has selected a competitor, it's not over.

Consider it time for your closing argument. This is your last chance to persuade the jury. They will deliberate upon what you say.

Here is a process for converting a lost-the-sale call into a won-the-sale call.

Note, this is *be real* time. If you don't *truly* believe in your software's value proposition, skip this step. You need to be able to speak from the heart.

Convene a final meeting

Convene a final meeting. Request, almost demand, a meeting with your primary contact, the ultimate decision maker, and as many purchasing team members as possible. When possible, meet in-person, but a conference call can also work.

Do not let them interrupt

You have nothing to lose (apparently you already lost) and everything to gain. It's time to drop everything you know about asking questions and listening. It's time to tell, tell, and tell!

Once convened, let them have it. Go up one side and down the other. Explain that while you appreciate that they have made a decision, you urge them to reconsider.

Do not let them interrupt.

Reiterate your value proposition

Reiterate your software's features and benefits, ROI, and overall value proposition.

Talk about their specific business problems and how your software is their solution. Restate the pain of the status quo.

Be confused and concerned

I once worked with Mariana Seldon. Mariana is a consistent top producer in a highly competitive software market. She sells software that manages direct mail marketing. As Mariana put it, "Our software puts addresses on envelopes. Or anything you want an address printed on for that matter. Lots of companies do what we do."

When I asked Mariana about her success, she said, "When a prospect tells me they are going with the competition, I respond by letting them know that I am confused. And I am concerned."

I asked her to go further as I wasn't quite sure how being confused and concerned helped her win sales.

Mariana tells them, "I'm confused. I don't understand how you could make that decision after all we've discussed. And I'm concerned for you."

Mariana said that this is where she goes up one side and down the other.

She says to them, "The last thing you need to do is send to duplicate addresses. In addition to being costly, it creates a lousy image for your company. Using our software, you can't mail to a duplicate address. If you miss a mail drop date, not only does it cost you money, you could lose your customer. Using our software, you can't miss a mail drop date."

Mariana said she then rattles off three or four of her prospect's major business challenges and explains how her software solves them.

Then she tells them, "I'm concerned. If you make the wrong decision, your mail costs will be higher, your database will be marginal, and your company will not gain the competitive advantage you need."

Mariana summed up her success in software sales, "I'm always confused and concerned!"

Use caring and conviction

When Mariana spoke, it was with conviction, but it was also with a caring attitude. She *truly* cared. Because of her belief in her software's value proposition, Mariana spoke from her heart. Even the tone of her voice and her body language exuded *the decision you made is not in your best interest; please reconsider.*

Leverage buyer's remorse

Buyer's remorse is a sense of regret that purchasing team members often have after making a decision. The costlier the software or the more impact the software will have on overall company operations, the higher the likelihood of buyer's remorse.

Play on it.

Early in my career, I received the dreaded call. I was working in the Boston office. My prospect was located two hours away in Portland, Maine.

My primary contact told me that his team had made a decision. They were going with the competition.

I met with all of them the following morning at 8:00am. (Early wakeup, long drive for me.)

I played on their buyer's remorse.

I spoke with passion about why they needed to consider making a new decision: buy my software, not the software they had decided to buy. I reiterated things that could go wrong when application software is implemented and how our company was one you could trust to not drop the ball. I created doubt about my competitor by recapping our competitive advantages.

I played on their buyer's remorse by questioning their selection criteria, expressing apprehension about implementing and using the competitor's software, and doggedly pleading for them to reconsider.

They did. I won the sale.

When all else fails, don't give up just yet. Make your closing argument. Your prospect may make a new decision and select your software. There is no *worst thing that can happen*. You already lost the sale.

Compete against yourself

Terry Anderson is a top producing software sales pro. While Terry likes to see her performance rankings against her peers, that is not what motivates her. Terry is more concerned about competing against herself. How she performed last quarter compared to how she performed this quarter is Terry's benchmark.

While it's great to be on the leaderboard (bragging rights, recognition, pride, etc.), what really counts to software sales pros is whether or not they are selling more now than they did before.

Use Terry's strategy. Compete against yourself.

- Are you better at selling today than you were yesterday?
- Is your personal sales activity goal higher this month than last month?
- Do you know more about your industry this quarter than you did last quarter?
- Is your commission check bigger this month than it was last month?

Importance of listening

"The single biggest problem in communication is the illusion that it has taken place."

— George Bernard Shaw

Every salesperson I've met thinks they are a good listener. I think I'm a good listener. We are all laboring under an illusion.

We can never stop improving our listening skills.

Here is the easiest, fastest way to improve your listening skills: shut up!

Allow for silent moments in your conversation. Ask open-ended questions. Then, be quiet. Pregnant pauses are okay. Prospects will either fill in the blanks or feel good that you are pondering their answers.

Other ways to improve your listening skills include the following:

- Listen with the intent to understand, not to reply.
- Question questions. When prospects ask a question, think for a moment. Do you understand why they are asking the question? If not, question their question. Ask for clarification.
- Repeat back what you think you heard before responding to questions. Whether prospects say *yes*, or *that's it*, or *what I meant was…* they will feel that they are being heard… that you are making an effort to understand them.
- Stop multitasking. Be in the moment.

When you listen to recordings of your conversations, I promise you, you are not going to believe how often you were tempted to, attempted to, or just plain talked over your prospect. I know because I think I'm a good listener. However, when I've listened to recordings of my conversations, I'm embarrassed to admit, I still need to work on my listening skills!

Learn prospect's KPIs

All businesses have key performance indicators (KPI). These are measurable indicators of success. The bottom line in business is revenue and profit, and KPIs drive revenue and profit.

Miscellaneous examples of KPIs include the following:

- New customers acquired
- Projects completed on time and in budget
- First time service call resolution
- Length of time to achieve new hire productivity
- Emails opened
- Mean time between product failure
- Cost of customer acquisition
- Inventory turns
- Existing customer business expansion

I've shared many top producer stories throughout this book when sales pros demonstrated their software's impact on prospects' KPIs. But I wanted to call out the importance of learning your prospects' KPIs separately.

When you understand how your prospects' track and measures success, you can connect the dots between improving your prospects' KPIs and your software. You gain a competitive advantage!

Dirty words

Your choice of language can distinguish you from competitors. For example, when prospects speak to your competitors, the competitors often refer to their company as a *vendor*. They schedule a software *demo* of their *features and functionality*. In your conversations, if you refer to your company as a *software company* and you schedule a *product tour* of your *software solution*, you have distinguished your company from competitors simply by selecting better language and avoiding *dirty words*.

Instead of this:	Use this:
Our customers are satisfied	Our customers are delighted
Vendor	Solution provider or software company
Bug fix	Software enhancement
Bug	Development opportunity
Programmer	Software developer
Spend time	Invest time
Problem	Business challenge
Customer service rep	Customer advocate or customer satisfaction

	representative
Cost, price, fee	Investment, total, sum
Contract	Agreement letter or paperwork
Project	Engagement
Signature	Approval or autograph
Demo	Software presentation, demonstration, or product tour
Touch base	Additional information for you

Provide additional information

Gaston Russi is an inside sales professional. His job is to intelligently manage his territory in order to identify and *reel in* qualified prospects.

"When I say *reel in*, I mean that after I identify a potential prospect, I keep in constant contact with her. Every email I send or voicemail I leave, I communicate new information that has value to my prospect," Gaston told me.

He keeps a list of "ten new pieces of information" that may be relevant to his prospects on a note by his phone. Gaston said he never *touches base* with his prospects.

"I hate *touch base*," he told me. "What does *touch base* mean anyway? When I communicate with my prospects, I want to add value. Every time my prospects hear from me, I provide them with new, useful information."

At the time I spoke with Gaston, the ten new pieces of information he had lined up included the following:

1. A press release regarding a new software update.
2. The result of a survey that is relevant to his software.
3. Quotes from industry pundits that support his software's value proposition.
4. More detailed information regarding a unique feature of his software.
5. A relevant article from an industry publication.
6. A summary of an interview with a leading industry executive, also supporting his software's value proposition.
7. An outline of the post-purchase implementation plan.
8. Bios of support team members.
9. A checklist of software features that prospects should be considering.
10. Complimentary tickets to an upcoming industry tradeshow

Leverage sales engineers

Sales Engineers (SE) are people who can explain the technicalities of your software. Titles may vary, but the Sales Engineer role is often crucial to selling complex or enterprise application software. Engineers take over the keyboard when it is necessary to dive deep into the how's and why's of your software functionality.

Leverage your Sales Engineers' expertise. Provide them with an executive summary of the software features that will be relevant to various purchasing team members. Let your SE know who's who. Provide him with guidance as to how he can best add value during your software demonstration.

SE's contributions to a software demonstration are often the reason why sales are won.

Quote their mission statement

Rocio Fonseca sells software website development services to nonprofit foundations (e.g. Bill and Melinda Gates Foundation, Robert Wood Johnson Foundation, The Pew Charitable Trusts). She is a top producer.

Rocio told me, "I read my prospects' quarterly reports. They always have a mission statement. I quote their mission statement during my software demonstration and show them how my software supports it."

Like Rocio, to be a top producer, tie your software's value proposition to your prospects' mission statements.

Conclusion

Selling software is an awesome career. It is lucrative and exciting. Every prospect presents you with an opportunity to learn, to help people solve real problems, and to make a lot of money.

Software sales is recession proof, too. No matter how sluggish the economy, there are always software companies in growth mode.

Depending on the software you sell, you sometimes have an impact on society as a whole. For example, software that helps healthcare providers, green manufacturers, biologists, educators, civil engineers, educational institutions, and the like benefit *all* of humanity.

Software companies tend to be highly profitable. Unlike a manufacturer, who makes a product, sells it, and then has to reproduce it to make another sale, when you sell software, you still have it. You can sell it a hundred times or a thousand times, and you don't have to remake it. Therefore, software companies can afford to invest in research and development, and provide better work environments and compensation for their employees.

When selling software, one of the biggest rewards isn't tangible. When you speak with your delighted customers after they're up and running and enjoying the benefits of your software, the feeling is moving.

Few careers offer so much diversity, opportunity for growth, and ongoing innovation.

I encourage you to use the tools in this book and go out and have fun selling even more software and making even more money!

Appendix A – Question Lists

What follows is a compilation of questions presented throughout the book. Some are question to ask prospects; others are questions to anticipate that purchasing team members will want answered.

Pre-demonstration discovery questions

Pre-demonstration discovery questions for three different software applications.

Master question list – when selling software to manage sales commissions

- Are reps paid on a salary plus commission?
- If commission only, is it paid monthly? Is it paid on cash receipts or bookings?
- Define the sales crediting process – how do you determine who gets credit for the sale? What *value* does the salesperson get credit for?
- Does commission kick in only after goal is achieved?
- How do you define sales territories?
- Do you calculate or pay incentives in more than one currency or language?
- Are sales managers paid an override?

Master question list – when selling software to manage a recruiting process

- Describe the information gathering process when you begin a recruiting assignment. Who does what? What bottlenecks do you experience? What steps of the process are frustrating or time consuming? How would reducing the frustration and time required impact productivity?
- How often do you use personalized, mass emails to communicate with your network (clients, candidates, potential clients, etc.?) What process is in place and how long does it take? What bottlenecks do you experience? Would mass email campaigns be effective if you do had the time? How would your business be impacted if you sent a personalized email to all your key contacts once per quarter?
- What tools do you currently have in place to maintain organized, consistent data? How are the tools working? Please rate your database for its integrity on a one to 10 scale, 10 being perfect. For any answer below a 10: What would it take to make it a 10?
- How does your firm share an updated list of all active search projects? What tools do you have to verify what each member has accomplished on a project or during a certain period? What percent of your time is consumed by these information-sharing tasks? What is the value of your time in dollars per hour?

Master question list – when selling software to manage a physician practice

- Do you need electronic medical records?

- Are you using a Windows platform?
- What areas of your practice would you identify as having workflow challenges?
- What requirements do you have for scanning?
- What common challenges do you incur with regard to remittance?
- Will you want any data converted from your old system to your new system?
- Any remote offices? If so, for what purpose?
- How do you do electronic posting?
- What percent of your patients are on Medicare?
- How much are couriers costing you? What courier challenges exist?
- How much are transcription services costing you? What challenges exist with regard to transcriptions?
- How much time (man-hours) is spent defending reimbursement rejections?
- What regulatory/compliance issues do you have?

It's worth noting that the majority of these questions are open-ended. They cannot be answered with a *yes* or *no*. When you use open-ended discovery questions, prospects provide richer answers.

Identify prospects' challenges

Discovery questions that enable you to understand prospects' challenges and level of need to solve those challenges.

Discovery Question	Reason for Question
How did you hear about our software solution?	Your questions and sales demonstration may change based on your lead source. For example, if the prospect was referred by someone he trusts, your conversation will be different from a prospect who found you via a Google search.
What causes you to be interested in our software solution at this point in time? *Depending on the answer, probe further: Why not wait six months? Why was this not so important six months ago?* *What would be the consequences if you do nothing and remain status quo?*	Identifies the level of urgency to buy your software.

Looking at the next two or three quarters, what are some of the other business initiatives taking place? *Where does investing in new software fall in importance compared to those initiatives?*	Further establishes level of urgency.
Please tell me about the business challenges that you would like to resolve. *For each challenge, consider asking:* • *Tell me more.* • *How many people deal with that?* • *How long does it take?* • *What is the workflow?* • *How do you determine when the challenge is resolved?* • *How can we calculate the cost of this process?* • *If the problem went away, how would it help?*	Enables you to demonstrate how to solve business challenges. Positions you as a consultative partner, not a vendor. Identifies the foundation for an ROI. Distinguishes you from competitors who do not ask these questions.
What type of information reporting do you need? *Why and when do you need it?*	Identifies which reports to demonstrate.

Ask your primary contact

Questions for your primary contact that will reveal his or her role and level of authority in the decision making process.

• How long have you worked at the company?
• How did you come to work here; did the company find you or did you find the company?
• Please tell me more about your responsibilities. What is your role in the software purchase process?
• Have you led the software purchasing process previously, here or at other companies?
• What software functionality will be most important to you?
• Who, *including you*, is involved in the decision making process?
• I noticed that you haven't included anyone from your _____ team. Who will be assessing that functionality of our software?

Ask individual purchasing team members

Questions to ask purchasing team members when you meet them individually. Time is limited, so carefully prioritize your questions.

- Please tell me about your key responsibilities.
- What is the most important aspect of this new software to you? Why?
- Compared to other important business initiatives you are managing over the next few quarters, what is the relative priority of implementing this new software?

Be prepared to answer purchasing team member questions

Questions you will be asked by purchasing team members, reflective of their roles on the purchasing team.

Ultimate decision maker

- Does purchasing software make business sense, financially and generally, at this point in time?
- Should this purchase be prioritized now?
- What options were considered?
- How will this software affect customers, investors/shareholders, and employees?

Primary contact

- What is this company's reputation for after-the-sale support?
- Am I providing purchasing team members with what they need to know in order to make a decision whether to buy?
- Can this software implementation be done now?
- How will this software affect my reputation, now and in the future?

Approvers

- How will my business day be better because of this software?
- How much of a headache will it be to start using this software?
- Is using this software advantageous to my career?
- How will this software make me, my department, or my boss more effective?

Tech dude

- Will this software introduce any security vulnerabilities?
- What requirements (personnel, technology, compliances, etc.) are necessary for us to support it? Is it in budget?
- Will it integrate smoothly with other applications?

- What are the qualifications of this company's support team members? What is the quality of their support?

Identify the software purchasing process

Questions that enable you to identify prospects' software purchasing process.

Questions	Reason for question
What criteria will you use to make your decision? *How will you determine which software solution is best for your situation?* *Depending on answer:* *How did you decide this is the most important criteria?* *Would you like some assistance creating an evaluation process?*	Identifies the decision-making criteria. Or, identifies there is no decision-making criteria, which puts you in a position to develop a partner relationship and assist with developing decision-making criteria. If you can participate in the creation of a software evaluation process, you can influence the opportunity in your favor.
Have you had to make similar purchases during your tenure with this company?	Identifies whether you will need to lead the purchasing process or let your primary decision maker lead the process.
Please tell me about your software purchasing process. *What are the next steps in your buying process?* *What takes place after you attend a software demonstration?* *Who needs to be involved in those steps?* *At which points in the process will you require approval to proceed and from whom?*	Identifies your prospects purchasing actions. Identifies purchasing team members who may not need to be involved in a demonstration, such as Legal or IT.
Who has responsibility for the financial	Identifies the status of the

decision regarding this purchase? *How will you assess your return-on-investment and/or evaluate the business case?* *How will you determine whether this purchase is within your budget?* *Will funds need to be reallocated from other budget items in order to purchase? How does that take place?* *If you do not create an ROI analysis, why would a senior executive approve this purchase?* *Would you like some help creating an ROI?*	cost justification, ROI, or business need justification.
Will a request for a proposal be created? *Is there a consultant involved?*	Identifies additional steps you may need to take in order to make the sale. You may have to respond to a proposal or you may have to interact with a consultant.
What other options are you considering to solve these problems? What is your familiarity with those options? *Is developing software in-house an option?* *What selection criteria have you established?* *How did you decide these are the most important criteria?* *How will you evaluate software against your selection criteria?* *Do you use any form of rating system to evaluate software?* *Would you like some assistance creating an evaluation process?*	Identifies the competitive nature of the opportunity.

Be prepared to answer risk mitigation questions

Questions you will be asked by purchasing team members regarding risk mitigation.

- Do I trust this vendor/salesperson to follow through on his commitments post-sale? If things go south during implementation, do I trust the salesperson to be my advocate post-sale?
- What is my TCO (Total Cost of Ownership)?
- How long before this technology becomes obsolete?
- What does adoption look like? What resources are necessary for successful implementation post-sale *and* what resources/processes need to be in place for ongoing successful operation?
- Even if I trust the vendor and the salesperson, do I trust our internal resources to implement successfully and to maintain success post-sale? How will the vendor help me with this process?
- What are the risks (to me/company/others) if this project fails? What are the benefits if it is successful?
- How do the above risks compare to (a) doing nothing (b) an alternative use of capital?

Ask post sale risk mitigation questions

Questions that will enable you to mitigate post-sale problems.

- Who will be responsible on your side for a successful implementation?
- Who is the ultimate owner of implementation success and post-implementation success?
- How much time can users allocate during training and implementation?
- What simultaneous initiatives may be in play that could affect our implementation schedule?

Appendix B – Software Demonstration Evaluation Form

Software Demonstration Evaluation

(Example, create your own)

	Needs improvement	Satisfactory	Excellent
Prospect: _____			
Planning			
Know *all* the purchasing team members	☐	☐	☐
Know *all* the needs (business problems to solve)	☐	☐	☐
Know the purchasing process	☐	☐	☐
Know where they are in the purchasing process	☐	☐	☐
Opening			
WIIFM (What's in it for my prospect?)	☐	☐	☐
Qualifications of team	☐	☐	☐
Agenda	☐	☐	☐
Time frame	☐	☐	☐
Additions to agenda	☐	☐	☐
Agreement on next step	☐	☐	☐
Body			
Memorable manner	☐	☐	☐
How software solves business problems	☐	☐	☐
Report usage	☐	☐	☐
Competitive knock-offs	☐	☐	☐
ROI analysis	☐	☐	☐
How to get started	☐	☐	☐
Close			
Life without solutions	☐	☐	☐
Agreement on next step & time frame	☐	☐	☐
Delivery			
Body language	☐	☐	☐
Success stories	☐	☐	☐
Vocal variety	☐	☐	☐
Visual aids	☐	☐	☐
Audience participation	☐	☐	☐
Completed within time limit	☐	☐	☐

Appendix C – Example of a Purchasing Team Member Profile

Title – Construction Site Engineer

Responsibilities	Proactively participate in OAC (owner, architect, contractor meetings)
	Write and track RFIs, manage RFI approval process
	Manage field administration with Engineers, Architect, Project Manager, and Supervisor
	Liaise between Project Manager and technical disciplines involved in a project
	Make sure project is executed per contract
	Manage field operations
	Receive equipment on time and make sure everything is installed on property
	Manage project controls, keep current drawing lists and sets
	Track who'll do what by when on myriad items, like change orders being distributed to the field; keep superintendent informed, special scheduling, and other day-to-day priorities
Day-in-the-life-of	Pressure to deliver on time and on budget
	Report to numerous people
	Try to complete or manage mundane matters so focus is on most important projects
	Maintain efficiency
	Achieve all the tasks necessary to accomplish in a day
	Extinguish unexpected fires
	Accomplish observable key performance indicators (KPIs tend to not be measurable)
Role on purchasing team	☐ Ultimate decision maker ☐ Primary contact ☐ Tech dude ☑ User ☐ Other _____
Software	Feature:

features & benefits	Ability to organize current document sets
	
	Benefits:
	
	    Prevent working off dated documents, mitigate disputes, save time
	
	Feature:
	
	    Version control tracking
	
	Benefits:
	
	    Keep all subcontractors up-to-date, catch mistakes, and easily access historic info
	
	Feature:
	
	    Issue creation and ongoing management
	
	Benefits:
	
	    Track issue resolution time to reward managers
	
	    Prevent anything from slipping through the cracks
	
	Feature:
	
	    2D and 3D document saving and file control for rapid access in the field
	
	Benefits:
	
	    Easy access control
	
	    Permissioning of folders for auditing purposes
	
	    Rapid approval of work flows

Communication style	Slow down, be measured

About the Author

Brian Geery's specialty is working with software companies to improve their demonstration-to-close ratio. Brian knows how to sell software. His high-growth software company clients attest to it.

Brian has a 25 plus year track record working with technology industry sales leaders to fine-tune their sales engines through the development and execution of successful sales strategies. He works alongside his clients to build scalable sales processes that deliver predictable revenue.

Brian has worked with more than 175 clients, including AT&T, Centerstone Software, Centric Software, CerTek Software, Comcast, Cornerstone Software, Drawbase Software, Fidelity Investments, Ford Motor Company, Genesys Software, Harvard Business Publishing, HP, Iron Mountain, LPA Software, Process Software, Radview Software, Thomson Investment Software, and TimeLinx Software.

Brian's strategies for sales success have been published in *Selling Power Magazine, Sales & Marketing Management Magazine, The Wall Street Journal*, and numerous sales publications and blogs. He has been a guest speaker on sales-related television and radio shows, and has been a featured speaker at a multitude of sales conferences. He is the co-author of *Buy Me, I'm Worth It!* and the publisher of the *SalesNv Blog*.

Prior to his career in consulting, Brian was a top producer in sales, sales management, and branch management at three technology companies over a 10-year period.

During his consulting career, he has served as Vice President of Sales & Service at four technology companies where he built scalable sales organizations from the low millions to the high millions, including one company that doubled sales three years in a row, and was consequently acquired for $360 million in cash.

As a proponent and advocate for the sales profession, Brian has held the following positions:

- Vice President of the Sales and Marketing Executives Association
- Vice President of the New England Technology Sales Executives Association
- Member of the Institute for the Ages Technology Circle
- President of the Sales and Marketing Toastmasters Association
- President of a condo association (a momentary lapse in sanity)

Services to Increase Software Sales

Buy book in quantity

If you're thinking of buying this book for a large group, contacts us for a better price. We can drop ship any quantity. Group purchases start at 10 books.

1 – 9 copies	No discount
10 – 99 copies	25% discount
100 – 249 copies	30% discount
250 – 499 copies	35% discount
500 and up	Contact us for a quote

Make It Your Own

Include your motto, mission, and logo on the outside and inside covers, even add a page with your personal message. We can also create a customer front and back cover for a fee. Please contact us (see below) to discuss customization details.

Consulting services

My firm, SalesNv, offers a variety of consulting and training services to increase software sales. Have a conversation with us.

Brian Geery

SalesNv.com

617.513.1923 (call or text)

bgeery@salesnv.com

Works Consulted

Beckwith, Harry. *Selling the Invisible: A Field Guide to Modern Marketing*. New York: Warner, 1997. Print.

Bens, Ingrid. *Facilitating with Ease!: Core Skills for Facilitators, Team Leaders, and Members, Managers, Consultants, and Trainers*. San Francisco, CA: Jossey Bass, 2005. Print.

Bertuzzi, Trish. *The Sales Development Playbook: Build Repeatable Pipeline and Accelerate Growth with inside Sales*. N.p.: n.p., n.d. Print.

Bosworth, Michael T., John R. Holland, and Frank Visgatis. *Customer Centric Selling*. New York: McGraw-Hill, 2010. Print.

Bosworth, Michael T. *Solution Selling: Creating Buyers in Difficult Selling Markets*. Burr Ridge, IL: Irwin Professional Pub., 1995. Print.

Carnegie, Dale. *How to Win Friends and Influence People*. London: Vermilion, 2006. Print.

Cohan, Peter E. *Great Demo!: How to Create and Execute Stunning Software Demonstrations*. New York: IUniverse, 2005. Print.

Cruikshank, Jeffrey L., and Arthur W. Schultz. *The Man Who Sold America: The Amazing (but True!) Story of Albert D. Lasker and the Creation of the Advertising Century*. Boston, MA: *Harvard Business Review*, 2010. Print.

Dixon, Matthew, and Brent Adamson. *The Challenger Sale: Taking Control of the Customer Conversation*. New York: Portfolio/Penguin, 2011. Print.

Eades, Keith M. *The New Solution Selling: The Revolutionary Sales Process That Is Changing the Way People Sell*. New York: McGraw-Hill, 2004. Print.

Freese, Thomas A. *Secrets of Question Based Selling: How the Most Powerful Tool in Business Can Double Your Sales Results*. Naperville, IL: Source, 2000. Print.

Gitomer, Jeffrey H. *Jeffrey Gitomer's Little Red Book of Selling: 12.5 Principles of Sales Greatness: How to Make Sales Forever*. Austin: Bard, 2004. Print.

Gschwandtner, Gerhard *works from multiple publications (books, articles, and videos)*.

Halligan, Brian, and Dharmesh Shah. *Inbound Marketing: Get Found Using Google, Social Media, and Blogs*. Hoboken, NJ: Wiley, 2010. Print.

Heiman, Stephen E., Diane Sanchez, Tad Tuleja, and Robert B. Miller. *The New Strategic Selling: The Unique Sales System Proven Successful by the World's Best Companies, Revised and Updated for the 21st Century*. New York: Warner, 1998. Print.

Holden, Jim. *Power Base Selling: Secrets of an Ivy League Street Fighter*. New York: Wiley, 1990. Print.

Holmes, Chet. *The Ultimate Sales Machine: Turbocharge Your Business with Relentless Focus on 12 Key Strategies.* New York: Portfolio, 2007. Print.

Hopkins, Tom. *How to Master the Art of Selling.* New York, NY: Warner, 1982. Print.

Johnson, Spencer, and Larry Wilson. *The One Minute Manager Salesperson.* London: HarperCollinsEntertainment, 2004. Print.

Konrath, Jill. *Agile Selling: Getting up to Speed Quickly in Today's Ever-changing Sales World.* N.p.: n.p., n.d. Print.

Levesque, Ryan. *Ask: The Counterintuitive Online Formula to Discover Exactly What Your Customers Want to Buy ... Create a Mass of Raving Fans ... and Take Any Business to the next Level.* N.p.: n.p., n.d. Print.

McCray, Vickie L. *How to Swim with the Sharks: A Survival Guide for Leadership in Diverse Environments.* Alexandria, VA: TP Rewards, 2014. Print.

Miller, Robert B., Stephen E. Heiman, and Tad Tuleja. *Strategic Selling: The Unique Sales System Proven Successful by America's Best Companies.* New York: W. Morrow, 1985. Print.

Parinello, Anthony. *Selling to VITO: The Very Important Top Officer.* Holbrook, MA: Adams Media, 1999. Print.

Pink, Daniel H. *To Sell Is Human: The Surprising Truth about Moving Others.* New York: Riverhead, 2012. Print.

Rackham, Neil. *SPIN Selling.* New York: McGraw-Hill, 1988. Print.

Riefstahl, Robert. *The New Demonstrating to Win!: The Indispensible Guide for Demonstrating Complex Products.* Colorado Springs, CO: Demonstrating to WIN, LLC., 2011. Print.

Roberge, Mark. *The Sales Acceleration Formula: Using Data, Technology, and Inbound Selling to Go from $0 to $100 Million.* N.p.: n.p., n.d. Print.

Ross, Aaron, and Marylou Tyler. *Predictable Revenue: Turn Your Business into a Sales Machine with the $100 Milion Best Practices of Salesforce.com.* West Hollywood, CA: PebbleStorm, 2012. Print.

Tracy, Brian. *The Psychology of Selling.* Nashville, TN: Thomas Nelson, 2007. Print.

Weinberg, Mike. *New Sales: Simplified.* New York: AMACOM, 2012. Print.

Ziglar, Zig. *Selling 101: What Every Successful Sales Professional Needs to Know.* Nashville: Thomas Nelson, 2003. Print.

CPSIA information can be obtained
at www.ICGtesting.com
Printed in the USA
FFOW01n0254281016
28863FF